TO THE ARCTIC

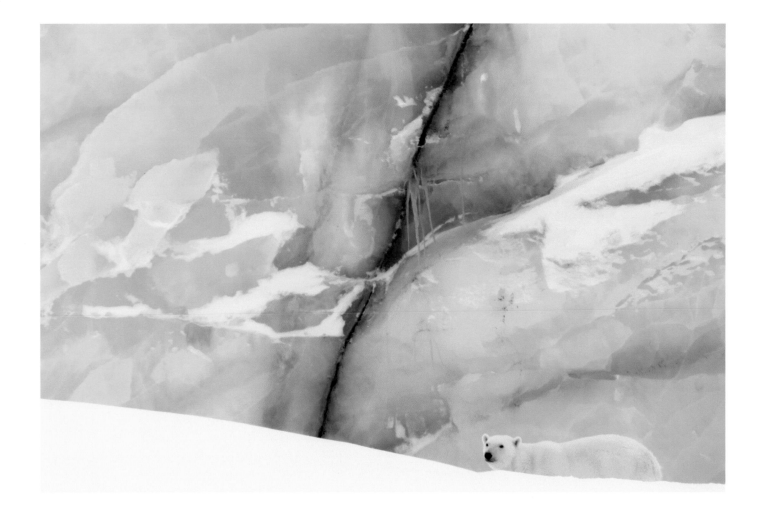

Photography by FLORIAN SCHULZ

Companion to The MacGillivray Freeman Film *To The Arctic* ▪ Foreword by Sylvia Earle

BRAIDED RIVER ▪ WITH SUPPORT FROM CAMPION FOUNDATION AND MARGOT MacDOUGALL

TABLE OF CONTENTS

For thousands of years, humans have found ways to respond to the challenges of living in the frozen world of the Arctic. But even the oldest human cultures in the far north have been preceded, by thousands of millennia, by creatures exquisitely adapted to a realm where water, the single nonnegotiable thing required for life, exists in all of its wondrous forms: as solid, gas, and liquid. Massive sheets of slowly rotating sea ice shield the heart of the Arctic—an ocean at the top of the world where life abounds, from the surface to the greatest depths more than three miles below.

This remarkable volume of Florian Schulz's photography, and the film it accompanies, is a celebration of Arctic life in its many resilient forms, with intimate glimpses of polar bears, foxes, walruses, caribou, and others who share with humans a common need for water, warmth, food, shelter—and protection from predators.

The miracle of life on Earth shines through in the images and stories presented here. For humans, the Arctic is a harshly inhospitable place, but the conditions there are precisely what polar bears require to survive—and thrive. "Harsh" to us is "home" for them. Take away the ice and snow, reduce the temperature by even a little, and the realm that makes their lives possible literally melts away.

Sadly, in our time, and largely by our actions, this is exactly what is happening. Owing primarily to consequences of the twentieth-century appetite for energy derived from burning coal, oil, and gas, coupled with global destruction of carbon dioxide–absorbing forests of the land, and plankton and other natural systems in the sea, Earth's atmosphere and ocean have been swiftly overloaded with carbon dioxide and methane. The results are visible in an unnatural warming of the world, rapid shifts in climate and weather, an inexorable rise in sea level, and a relentless trend toward acidification of the ocean.

The use of fossil fuels served us well during the past century, driving a technological revolution, increasing farm yields, and powering transportation and communication systems. But the most important gift derived from the use of fossil

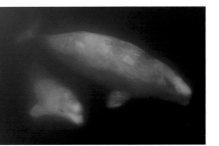

There are limits
to what we can do
to the natural systems
that keep us alive,
no matter where we are
on the planet.

fuels has nothing to do with new "miracle" materials, medical breakthroughs, or urban infrastructure. It has everything to do with insights gained by being able to fly high in the sky, to see the world as a tiny blue speck in an otherwise inhospitable universe, and to communicate the knowledge thus gained to everyone, everywhere.

Now we know what was impossible to grasp prior to the end of the twentieth century. And now, at the beginning of the twenty-first, we can use our distinctly human capacity to gather information, grasp the patterns, anticipate the outcomes, and take actions that are in our best interests. We have an edge when it comes to ensuring a long and enduring future for ourselves, because we are capable of understanding that we must change our ways. The animals do not have the ability to understand why the changes are taking place, and even if they did, they would not know how to stop them. But we do know why, and what to do about it: there are limits to what we can do to the natural systems that keep us alive, no matter where we are on the planet.

Our fate is intimately linked to that of the natural systems that provide the foundation for our economies, our security, our health, and, ultimately, our very lives. Now we know that the time to act is shrinking, coincident with the diminishing fabric of life on the land and in the sea—and the loss of polar ice and snow.

There is time, but not a lot, to shift our way of thinking—and acting. By celebrating the Arctic, the contributors to this book and the accompanying film convey a message of urgency laced with hope. There is time, but not a lot, to shift our way of thinking, to protect the Arctic as if our lives depend on it—because they do.

Oceanographer Dr. Sylvia Earle is Explorer-in-Residence at the National Geographic Society, and leader of the Sustainable Seas Expeditions. Her proposal to save and restore "the blue heart of the planet" received a TED prize. She is chief advisor to One World One Ocean, a global campaign to restore and protect the world's oceans.

◄ An ice floe miles from shore is the only place for a polar bear mother and her cub to rest as the summer progresses. Barents Sea, Norway.

▲▲ Beluga whales in Hudson Bay, Canada. ▲ A bearded seal on the coast of Alaska. ◄ A walrus peeks out of the sea ice on the Barents Sea.

In forty-five years of producing films, many of which have been about the oceans or in remote regions of the world, I was still unprepared for what I found in the Arctic. In the far north, everything exists on a grand scale—the sky seems to stretch into eternity, the mountains, valleys, and ice fields make for landscapes and seascapes of out-sized proportions. Which is perhaps why I was immediately attracted to the Arctic as a topic for a story told in IMAX® Theatres, the biggest in the world.

There are grand and fascinating Arctic stories worth telling on the giant screen. In Alaska's Arctic National Wildlife Refuge, on Alaska's north coast, more than 190 species of birds from six continents and all fifty states come to nest and rear their young. Waterfowl, raptors, shorebirds, gulls and terns, owls and songbirds, some traveling to the Arctic from as far away as Argentina, Africa, and New Zealand, rely on the Arctic. Hundreds of thousands of caribou or reindeer, who once roamed the Arctic with woolly mammoths and saber-toothed cats, today still follow their ancient migrations. Their pathways through mountains and across rivers are carved into the landscape. Beneath the ice in the Arctic, algae clings to the ice which feeds the plankton animals that feed fish, squid, and krill, which in turn feed whales and seals that feed polar bears and also the Inuit people who call the Arctic home.

Our journey to capture this majestic place on film took us to three countries over four years. But it was when we were just nine degrees shy of the North Pole aboard the icebreaker *Havsel* out of Svalbard, Norway, that the Arctic story we were about to tell finally revealed itself. It was our seventh expedition above the Arctic Circle. We had already captured a stunning array of land, bird, and sea life on film, yet nothing had prepared us for what we were about to witness.

It was 3:45 a.m. and the polar bear family we'd been watching in shifts was napping under the midnight sun. Earlier that day, this surprisingly trusting mother polar bear allowed our Zodiac to drift to within thirty feet of the ice floe where her two seven-month-old cubs frolicked like puppies, batted ice chips around like hockey pucks, pounced on each other in mock attacks, and sweetly nursed. As she did every

The Arctic ecosystem is in hot water. Perched atop the Arctic food chain, the world's largest land carnivore is poised to fall hard.

fifteen minutes or so, the sleepy mother bear lifted her muzzle to scan the air with a sniff of her nasal radar. Suddenly she was up. Approaching fast was a male polar bear—very thin and surely hungry this year. With a warning bark, the courageous mother bear sent her cubs scurrying into the water ahead as she dove in behind them to block the male bear during what became a grueling four-mile swim. Snarling and snapping whenever he got close, she finally stopped to make a stand, growling as if to say, "If you want to kill my cubs, you'll have to kill me first." Finally, the male bear turned away, ending the longest and most thrilling chase I have ever captured on film.

For five days and nights we enjoyed our status as the mother bear's adopted guests while she worked to feed and shelter her cubs among the ice floes. She never threatened us or tried to depart from us unless her cubs were under attack by an approaching male. In fact, her acceptance of our presence was something no bear biologist we spoke to had ever heard of before. Maybe part of this was filmmaker's luck, but it was probably more likely that our unthreatening proximity kept the desperate but wary male bears a few steps farther away from the savvy mother's cubs. Regardless of why this happened, these remarkable behaviors are helping us get a clearer picture of the state of the great white north.

The fact is the Arctic ecosystem is in hot water. During our twenty-two days in the Svalbard archipelago, we counted 132 bears when we should have counted only 30. This is because the widespread loss of sea ice had crowded bears normally spread over an area of fifty square miles into an area just ten miles square. With warming here accelerating faster than anywhere else, the fragile Arctic environment is the most precariously balanced on our planet. Nowhere is this rendered more vividly than in the daily struggle of the polar bear. Perched atop the Arctic food chain, with a two-thirds decline in population expected over the next forty years, the world's largest non-aquatic predator is likely to disappear entirely by the end of the century without greenhouse gas mitigation. And these magnificent creatures aren't the only ones global warming is pushing into a corner.

◄ A mother polar bear rests with her cubs on the ice of the Barents Sea.

▲ Polar bear tracks imprinted on snow. ◄ A polar bear pauses at the edge of an ice floe. Svalbard, Norway.

The Arctic Ocean is much more than a mysterious realm of ice and snow, if we take the trouble to look. It may be the world's smallest ocean, but it also serves as the thermometer at the top of our world. With average temperatures rising three times faster than anywhere else on the planet, its once-permanent summer ice pack is shrinking at an alarming rate. In fact, it is predicted that by 2035 this vital summer sea ice will be nonexistent for the first time in hundreds of thousands of years. With much of the krill and plankton feeding the oceanic food chain born beneath it, and with its cold freshwater runoff supercharging the currents of the Great Ocean Conveyor Belt that moderates weather everywhere, and with the polar ice pack acting as a climate-balancing shield that reflects 80 percent of the sun's energy back into space, it is easy to grasp how changes accelerating here will affect not just the Arctic environment but the rest of the world in significant ways beyond the foreseeable future.

Balancing the message between what is amazingly present in the Arctic ecosystem and what it is we are beginning to lose inspired the forty-five men and women crew members who joined my son Shaun (the film's producer) and me to endure subzero temperatures, hurricane winds, mosquito swarms thick as London fog, and endless hours of patient waiting.

In Alaska's Arctic, we focused on the Porcupine River caribou migration, where 110,000 of these majestic creatures pour through the mountain passes of Alaska's North Slope to birth calves that must be ready to outrun hungry wolves within minutes of their new hooves

hitting the ground. One magical misty morning our patient film crew awoke to find a herd serenely sauntering past their tent flaps, and quickly grabbing their cameras shot some wonderful close-ups.

To capture the diverse panoply of life under the sea ice in Canada's Arctic, we dove into the subfreezing arctic brine with our 400-pound submersible IMAX camera through a hole bored in the four-foot-thick surface ice. As risky as cave diving, this experience has the added danger that within forty-five minutes your hands will freeze stiff, your brain will numb to a crawl, and you'd better be finding the exit hole soon. Our film footage reveals a surprisingly colorful world of red and yellow anemones haunted by the lumbering grace of whale sharks, diving polar bears, and curiously playful walruses.

Cinematographers Bob Cranston, Brad Ohlund, Jack Tankard, Adam Ravetch, Howard Hall, along with Shaun and me, were all key to capturing these images so we could tell this important story. Photographer Florian Schulz, whose beautiful images are captured in the pages of this book, has worked many years to tell the Arctic story, to bring it to audiences who will never visit the Arctic yet should know and understand its beauty and relevance. Florian's camera artistry has taken Arctic imagery to a new height, and I believe he's currently the most imaginative wildlife photographer around.

And none of it can continue to be documented if the Arctic doesn't remain what it is. I am worried the polar bears are fighting a losing battle without our help. They, and all the other creatures that call

this realm their home, depend on the sea ice that gives the Arctic its unique and vital character, and its pivotal role in the greater dynamic of Earth. Without this ice, which human behaviors are causing to melt, what chance do this mother bear's cubs have, even if they manage to survive into adulthood? Without the ice, can there even be an Arctic?

And yet, as the spirit of our film *To The Arctic* and its beautiful companion book attest, I am hopeful. I am not alone in believing that with open eyes and hearts, and reasonable sacrifice, we can stop the damage, and even reverse some of it, before it's too late. But we need everyone—you—to do what you can to give this mother bear and her two cubs a future by caring about and saving their home. That is what we hope to inspire with *To The Arctic,* the first film to come out as part of our even larger One World One Ocean campaign, which aims to restore the health of our world oceans. As filmmakers and photographers, as storytellers, as grandparents, mothers, and fathers, we don't want to tell our children about this realm of ice at the top of our world by starting with the words "Once upon a time . . . . "

Greg MacGillivray has produced and directed more than thirty-five films for IMAX Theatres and other giant-screen cinemas and has twice been nominated for an Academy Award. He is president of MacGillivray Freeman Films and chairman of One World One Ocean Foundation, a nonprofit organization dedicated to changing the way people see and value the ocean.

◄ A playful cub keeps busy with a piece of ice. Nordaustlandet, Svalbard, Norway.

▲ Male polar bear searching the ice for seals. Barents Sea.

◄Coastal glaciers in northwestern Greenland.

It is March in northwestern Greenland, a time of transition between eternal night and everlasting sun. I am sitting on a *qamutiq*, an Inuit dogsled, at the edge of the Arctic Ocean, staring across the frozen fjord, awaiting the rise of the moon. A faint orange glow reflected in thin clouds promises its arrival. Sparkling stars fill the sky and the freezing air stings the bare skin on my face. The dogs that have so faithfully pulled us here are sleeping, curled up tightly against the cold. The deep silence is broken only occasionally by the cracking of the ice shifting with the tides. As I sit here in this utterly remote spot, my thoughts flash back to the places my passion for wilderness has taken me and the wildlife I have seen. With my inner eye I once again meet the enormous polar bear that pierces my soul with his powerful stare; I stand so close to a mother bear nursing her two cubs that I can hear their suckling noises; I see a myriad of birds return to their nesting ground in spring and the Arctic plains dotted with tens of thousands of caribou.

I have always been driven by a tremendous passion for wild places. Growing up in Germany, I became acutely aware of the distinct lack of wilderness around me and developed a deep appreciation for untouched land. A landscape free of human imprint speaks to me of something ancient, something real. In the vast Arctic wilderness we humans can be reminded of a world that existed before we dominated this planet. This alone is worth preserving. Years ago, I heard some politicians call the Arctic a barren wasteland, a flat white nothingness, implying that it is good only for exploitation. I knew then that I wanted to provide a different account to the world. These statements fueled my desire to explore and thoroughly document the Arctic from all angles—the air, the land, the ice, and the sea—so that I could show others what I knew to be extraordinary about this place. In the process I hoped I could change some minds about the Arctic and contribute to its protection.

~

Not seeing these creatures does not mean that they are not there, or that they do not need the land. They are all part of an interconnected web of life.

A loud crack in the ice snaps me out of my thoughts, and the bitter cold hits me again. The large orange moon hangs just above the mountains. From behind I hear soft steps. It is my wife, Emil, all bundled up in a thick parka, polar bear pants, and *kamik*—thick boots of polar bear fur that our Inuit guide has given us to protect against the cold. She climbs onto the plates of sea ice that form a pressure ridge at the edge of the fjord and looks up at the moon. I walk over to join her.

What we are looking over certainly can be seen as a flat white nothingness. But to me, it is nature's unspoiled canvas that the moon colors with its light. Our Inuit guide may see the seal lairs hidden in the ice and a fjord filled with narwhal in summer. If I think of other places in the Arctic that I have seen, I know that the image of a "barren wasteland" could not be further from the truth. Instead, I picture the golden tundra teeming with tens of thousands of caribou or think of the millions of birds that undertake incredible migrations to build their nests in this distant land. How we see the Arctic is clearly a matter of perspective. What once was simply a mysterious place on a map for me has become a place I have fallen in love with. Here, I have witnessed some of the most dramatic landscapes, the most spectacular light, the most memorable wildlife encounters, and the most awe-inspiring migrations that I have ever seen. The Arctic has lost not a bit of its mystery for me. It is true, however, that one can go days without many signs of life. During the last two days, as the sled dogs pulled us across the ice, I have seen only a raven following us and the odd track of an Arctic fox. I spent years exploring the high Arctic before I saw the big caribou herds or a polar bear. But I didn't give up. I felt I needed to put in the time until I was invited in to witness some of the spectacles the Arctic has to offer. What I know from my experience, and what I hope to share with those who may think of the Arctic as a nothingness, is that not seeing these creatures does not mean that they are not there, or that they do not need the land. They are all part of an interconnected web of life.

▲ The ice forms patterns where a piece of glacier has frozen into the Arctic Ocean.

◀ The moon rises over eastern Svalbard, Norway.

When MacGillivray Freeman Films asked me to be the photographer for the companion book to their film *To The Arctic*, I swallowed hard and had to think about it for a moment. At that point I had been photographing across the North American Arctic for several years, gaining valuable experience, but I knew this would be a enormous undertaking. Documenting the Arctic ecosystem for this book meant facing huge challenges: blizzards and extreme cold, remote locations, and changing sea ice conditions, not to mention the millions of mosquitoes present during summer. I knew it would be intense, but I was driven by my desire to explore some of the most remote Arctic regions and to get to know more of their wildlife. The film project connected with my belief in the importance of creating a visual account of a region that is so severely affected by climate change.

The body of work in this book is the result of many expeditions that I undertook over the course of six years, logging a total of fifteen months in the Arctic. I have journeyed more than twenty-five hundred miles on snow machines across the Arctic; traveled in traditional ways with Inuit guides and their sled dogs for hundreds of miles; visited Inuit communities from Point Hope, Alaska, to Qaanaaq,

Greenland; dove and snorkeled in the Arctic Ocean; spent over one hundred hours photographing from airplanes; rafted down Arctic rivers; camped among tens of thousands of migrating caribou; and accompanied the MacGillivray Freeman film team on an ice-going vessel in the middle of drifting pack ice.

As the photographs in this book guide you through the arc of a year, I sincerely hope that you'll marvel at the incredible diversity, richness, and value of this part of our planet. Perhaps if a certain image makes you pause, you will close your eyes and let your imagination wander to this mysterious, faraway place. You may fall in love with it, as I did. You may also sense, however, that underlying every image is a certain urgency—to look, to pay attention, to care.

~

I once dreamed of being a hunter, and wanted to learn from Native people how to read the ways of wildlife and the land. It was always about more than the kill; it was about my fascination with getting close to animals in the wild. Over the years I have followed my dream and have become a hunter of a different kind. With my camera I hunt for wildlife and for the light that falls over the

landscape. I hunt for rare experiences. Now, here in Greenland, I have traveled out with one of the last Inuit hunters—he looking for seals, I for images. I set up my tripod at the edge of the ice and marvel at this dreamlike scene. The moon and the vast landscape seem to look back at me with a smile. I feel insignificant and humble, knowing that I can survive the cold only under my thick polar bear skin, while the creatures that make the Arctic their home are perfectly adapted to a place that can seem so unforgiving. Perhaps it is this that makes me feel all the more alive and draws me back to the Arctic, time after time. As I stand here at what feels like the edge of the world, I hope that what I have documented over the past years will not simply become historic images, of something that once was. Humans have always been so ingenious. I hope we can bring about change so that the Arctic landscape, with its king the polar bear, can survive and still be witnessed by generations to come.

———

Florian Schulz has promoted establishing wildlife corridors for over a decade through his Freedom to Roam® projects in partnership with Braided River. He uses photography to instill a greater interest in and understanding of the importance of protecting wild habitats.

▲ A polar bear hides from an approaching male behind a snowdrift. Svalbard, Norway.   ►► The rising moon glows orange over northern Greenland.

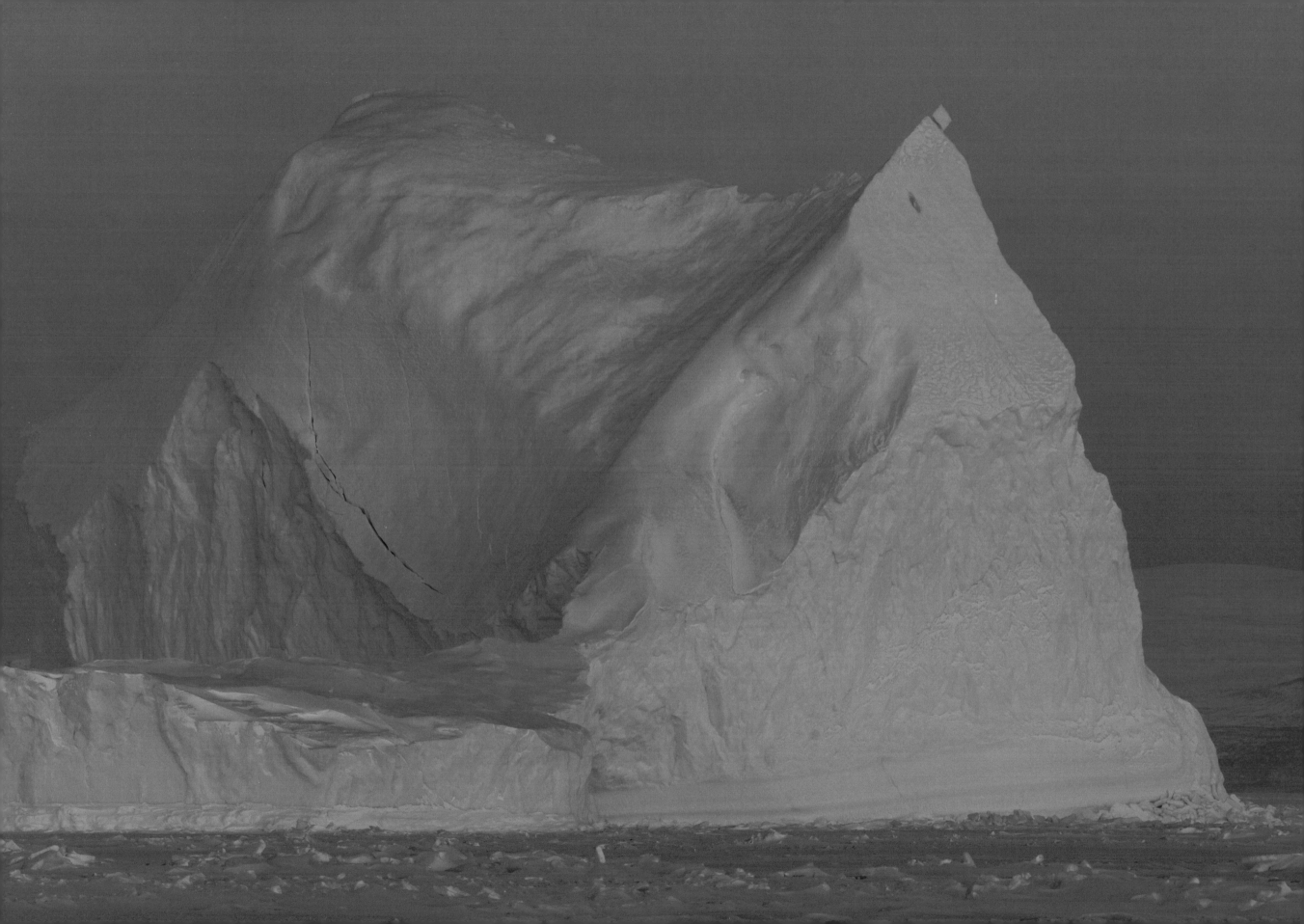

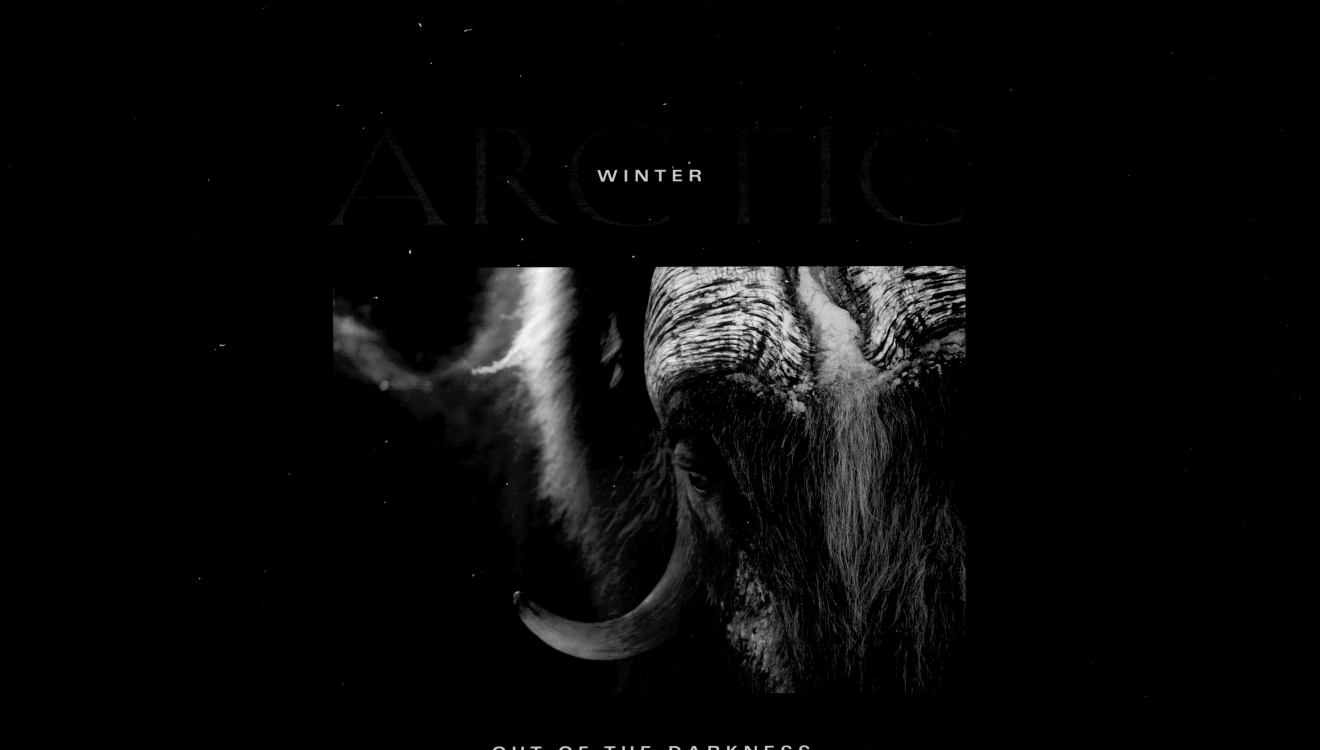

WINTER

ARCTIC

OUT OF THE DARKNESS

As winter arrives, the sun retreats farther south with every sunrise and sunset. It withdraws its warming rays and gives way to the polar night that lays its frozen grip over the Arctic. A blanket of snow covers the land, and the ocean begins to freeze. While much of nature falls dormant, this is a time of renewal for the ocean ice, which is the basis for most of the life in the Arctic Ocean. On this ice, seals haul out and give birth to their young in late winter. Because the seal pups cannot survive in the freezing water after birth, this ice is crucial to them. It is also the hunting platform for polar bears. Colder is better in the Arctic. The ice that builds up in winter needs to last well into spring and summer. To the animals that live here year round, such as the musk oxen, the cold is as normal as the air they breathe. They are perfectly adapted to the harsh Arctic environment.

By the winter solstice, darkness has reached its climax. North of the Arctic Circle the sun's rays vanish for at least twenty-four hours. Yet, near the circle a warm orange glow can still be observed toward the south at midday. This lingering twilight is the only reminder that the sun has not disappeared altogether from the planet. The long winter nights set the stage for a true wonder of the far north—the aurora borealis, which needs the darkness to unfold its breathtaking show. In reds, greens, and blues it dances across the Arctic sky until twilight chases it away.

◄◄ Preceding pages: Dripping water sculpts the ice inside a glacier. Svalbard, Norway. / A musk ox bull at sunrise. Northwest Alaska.

◄ The northern lights over the Tombstone Range. Yukon, Canada.

▲ Musk ox bulls are silhouetted against the sunrise. Northwest Alaska.

◄ Musk oxen gather on the exposed side of a mountain, where the harsh wind carries away the snow and allows easier access to food. Northwest Alaska.   ▲ The eyes of these female musk oxen reflect the white landscape around them.

MUSK OXEN

My eye is glued to the viewfinder as I watch every move of a big musk ox bull who is surrounded by his harem some fifteen yards in front of me. His massive head fills the whole frame. I am hunkered down on the ground, resting my telephoto lens on the frozen rocks. The bull's eyes are studying me in return. Above them curl powerful horns, bleached and cracked and resembling the weathered branches of a thousand-year-old tree. There is something ancient about these animals, as if they are survivors from a prehistoric time.

It has taken me several days to get close to the musk oxen. I have learned to stay close to the ground—often lying on my stomach and sliding closer foot by foot—because my low profile is less intimidating to them. I want to prevent them from stampeding and burning valuable energy.

Generally, however, their instinct tells them to stay put. Everything about them is designed to conserve energy. Instead of fleeing when threatened, they form a tight group, with their heads facing out and the calves placed in the center for protection. Sometimes, however, musk oxen are less docile and defensive and may attack in a stampede, or a lone bull will charge to protect the herd. I try to read the bull in front of me, attempting to anticipate how he will react to me.

He seems fine with my presence and goes back to herding his harem. As I lie there, I start to wonder what these animals survive on. No matter where I look, there is not a tree, a bush, or even a blade of grass in sight. I see only loose rocks covered by windblown snow. What could they possibly find here that would sustain their large bodies?

The bull has now circled the group of cows and drives them a bit in my direction. I see a few subordinate bulls mixed in with the group. The cows are reluctant to move much but form a line and are eyeing

◀ Musk ox bulls silhouetted against the orange sky of the rising sun. Northwest Alaska.

me with great curiosity. Against the dark backdrop of their bodies their eyes shine, reflecting the snow-white landscape. Their gently curling horns further accent their faces.

~

The next day I get up well before sunrise to search for the musk oxen. It is a clear day, and I hope to include the sun in some of my compositions. To my surprise I cannot find the group where they had been just the night before. With my binoculars I search the surrounding hilltops, but do not see even a single animal. I climb a low mountain to get an even broader view, but still nothing. I start growing anxious because along the northeast horizon a bright orange glow announces that the sun will be up soon. This far north, though, dawn and dusk seem to last forever at this time of the year, so I know I still have a bit of time to find the animals before the sun is up. I decide to go back to the same location I was the day before and walk over to the far side of the mountain, the only place where I have not already looked because it is very steep. The wind begins to pick up as I head down the slope. To my great surprise, I suddenly find the entire group. Why would they be in what seems to be one of the worst places in the

area, where the wind beats against the face of the mountain with the greatest strength? As I sit down and watch, I find the answer. The musk oxen dig away the shallow snow to get to the lichens that lie below. With every kick of their hooves, the strong wind carries the snow away, allowing the musk oxen to get to their food without expending valuable energy. And because of the wind, this face of the mountain never gets covered by more than a few inches of snow. As the sun starts to peek over the horizon, I pull out my wide-angle lens and carefully frame the entire group just as the hair of the musk oxen begins to glow with the first rays.

~

The next day the clear skies prevail but the wind picks up by the hour. I spend most of the middle of the day in a protected valley, waiting for the more dramatic light of the evening. As the sun moves toward the horizon I head back to the windblown ridges, where the musk oxen face the weather undeterred. The temperature is dropping, and the wind chill makes it feel much colder than twenty below zero. Now the wind becomes visible as it picks up snow crystals and blows them across the tundra. Leaning against the wind,

I near a group of bulls and find myself wishing for a musk ox's coat to protect me from the weather. Their long guard hair hangs from their bodies like beautiful overcoats. Underneath, their wool is eight times warmer than the highest-quality sheep wool.

I feel the gripping cold, especially on my face, where the snow crystals lash my skin like grains of sand. But I am excited about this turn in the weather. It allows me to create photographs that show a true Arctic scene, with conditions these musk oxen have to withstand many times in the course of the year.

The wind becomes so intense that the animals almost disappear behind a curtain of blowing snow, their long hair rippling around them like soft cloth. I try to get close enough to capture their image before the sun dips behind the ridgeline. Dropping to my knees, I frame the scene as the last rays cast pink light on the musk oxen's fur.

Then something magical happens. Three bulls take off from the group, heading directly toward the setting sun. For an instant they are in perfect formation. The blowing snow is so thick that it makes the three bulls seem to float magically above the ground. A photograph of a lifetime—and worth everything I had to endure to get it.

▶ Musk ox bulls walk through a blizzard toward the setting sun. Northwest Alaska.

▲ In late winter, the Western Arctic caribou herd begins its trek north. Northwest Alaska.

▲The short-legged Svalbard reindeer are only found on the Svalbard islands of Norway.

▲ An Arctic fox rests on a steep mountainside. Svalbard, Norway.

▲ Snowdrifts are sculpted by harsh wind and blowing snow. Svalbard, Norway.

▲ The face of the Negrebreen Glacier runs for twelve miles along the edge of the sea. Svalbard, Norway.

THE KINGDOM OF
THE POLAR BEAR

For days my guide and I have been searching for polar bears on the frozen plains of Norway's eastern Svalbard—Europe's largest wilderness. Imagine a high Arctic archipelago, roughly the size of West Virginia, covered with steep mountains and thick glaciers and located only about six hundred miles from the North Pole. I have been transported into a completely different world. There are no signs of life. It is as if the entire Earth has frozen solid. Walls of ice define the coastline and lead north toward the horizon as far as the eye can see. So far, our search has been fruitless; we have found only tracks. They seem to come out of nowhere and then disappear into the white, frozen world. It is a mystery to me how these large animals can elude us so easily.

A huge piece of a glacier wall that broke off and drifted about two miles out to sea in the fall is now frozen into the landfast ice. Towering some forty feet over the frozen ocean, it is an ideal place for a lookout. After I walk halfway around the iceberg, I find a spot where I am able to climb to the top. There, I kneel down and rest my binoculars on a tripod. The binoculars need to be completely steady if I want to find a white bear in this snow-covered landscape. Suddenly, I spot a speck in the distance. Squinting, I try to detect movement. As my excitement grows, I take slow breaths and blow the hot air down my chin so that the binoculars don't fog up. Then I can clearly see it—a polar bear is weaving its way through the pack ice. Even though the bear appears to be the size of an ant, it looks majestic, and a chill runs down my spine.

~

(to page 43)

▶ A polar bear wanders by a large piece of a glacier that has frozen into the sea ice. Svalbard, Norway.

▲ A mother polar bear sniffs the air as her cubs rest on a piece of glacier ice frozen into the Arctic Ocean. Baffin Island, Canada.

(from page 40)

It is close to three in the morning and the wind is picking up. The last rays of the sun turn the snowflakes into golden dust that settles over the Arctic landscape. It is time for us to go back to our camp and get some sleep. At least one of us will sleep; the other needs to be on polar bear watch, especially after finding fresh tracks on our way back to camp.

A large, flat iceberg gives us some good wind protection as long as the northeastern winds prevail. We silently go through our routine. With a hammer I break off some glacier ice so we can melt it for drinking water. We eat a bit of warm food before my guide crawls into his sleeping bag. Armed with a flare gun and with a rifle nearby, I begin my shift, sitting on top of the small berg and watching for any movement. It does not take long before my eyelids grow heavy. I am completely exhausted. The only thing I want to do is fall asleep, yet I am fascinated by this landscape. In some areas, especially close to shore, the ocean has frozen over during calm days. There, the surface is flat and smooth and the ice is bound to the land. In other areas, however, the ice cover looks more like an impenetrable boulder field. Ocean currents and storms push ice sheets together like tectonic

plates until the enormous force piles the ice up like miniature mountain ridges. They burst, crack, and collapse, creating an ice labyrinth. In some of the cavities, seals find shelter and give birth to their pups. Polar bears know this and regularly patrol this pack-ice jungle.

The next night my guide and I decide to leave our snowmobiles behind and explore the area on foot. Suddenly we come upon a fresh polar bear track. Might it belong to the bear from the day before, I wonder. We immediately look up and search around us, but here in the pack ice it is hard to make out anything. We look for a place to get a better view, and then we see the bear coming. It must have caught wind of our scent, but as far as we can tell, it has not yet seen us. It circles around to a more open area of ice and then continues zigzagging toward us, constantly probing the air with its nose. I am in complete awe. Here I am with one of the largest, most powerful land predators on Earth.

I drop to my knees and adjust my camera. Now I can see this magnificent animal through the lens. Its sheer size makes its eyes look like little black buttons. With powerful strides, the bear walks across the ice, then suddenly freezes. It sees us and continues on,

heading directly toward us. I carefully frame the image and take the first picture. The bear comes closer. Moment by moment it grows larger in my viewfinder. The images are spectacular. Again and again, I open the eye that is not looking through the lens to reassure myself of the distance. We start to talk to the bear. "Hey, you, what are you up to?" I say in a deep, friendly voice. I have practiced this with grizzlies, who normally move away when they hear my voice, but the polar bear does not even flinch. He just keeps coming. Now we are more assertive: "Hey, bear, that's close enough!" I shout. We can't let this bear get any closer. But I can't resist; I look through my camera lens once more. The bear seems to be looking straight into my eyes with a determined expression as it puts one paw in front of the other. *Click, click.* It is the moment I have been waiting for—one paw up in the air. Then two explosions break the silence. I am ripped out of my connection with this incredible animal. The bear bolts a few hundred feet, then stops. To our surprise, it turns toward us again. Now I am getting a bit nervous. We have used our "magic weapon," the big flare gun, but the bear is unfazed. We know then that it is time to get out of there. Sometimes photographs have to wait.

▲ A polar bear mother leads her cubs away from their denning area and onto the sea ice. Baffin Island, Canada.

▲ Polar bear cubs follow their mother across Wijdefjorden in search of seals. Svalbard, Norway.

▲ Cubs touch noses to reaffirm the close bond with their mother. Svalbard, Norway.

◄ A polar bear patrols the sea ice along the coast of eastern Svalbard, Norway.

▲ Curiosity leads a large male polar bear very close to the photographer.

▲ View of the coastline from the sea ice. Svalbard, Norway.

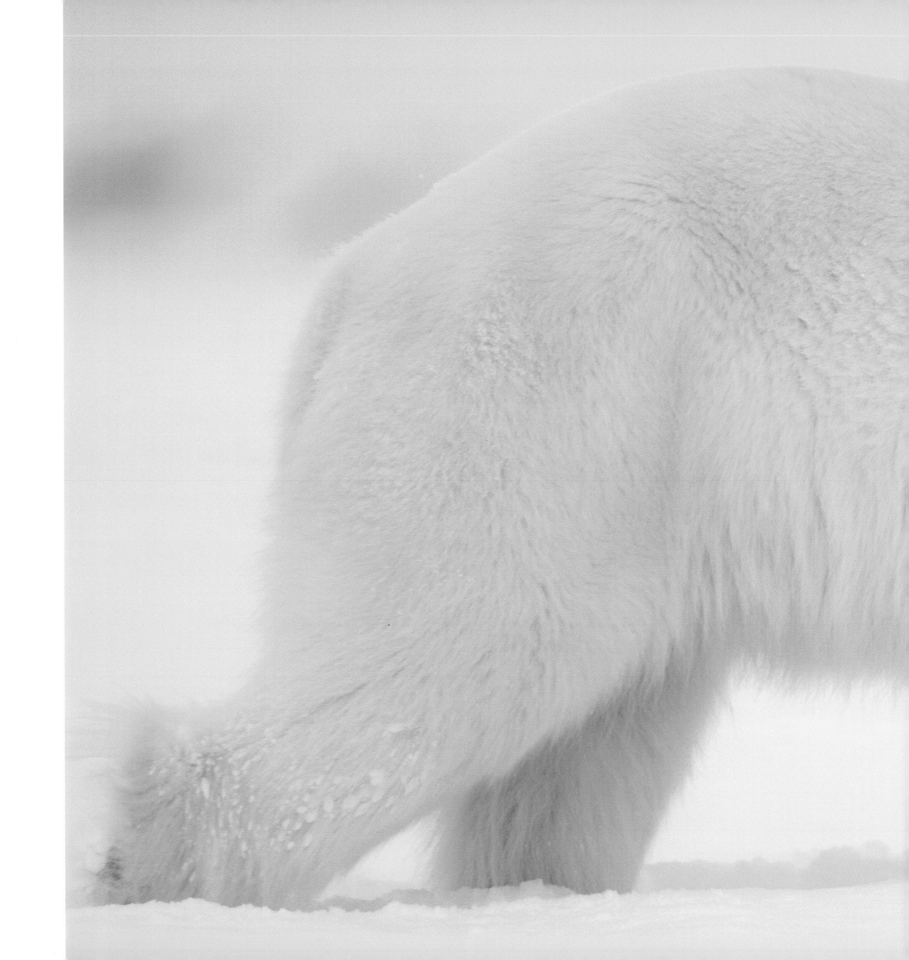

► A large male polar bear follows the tracks of a female during mating season.

► ► A female polar bear (right) fights a male that has been following her in an attempt to mate. Svalbard, Norway.

◄◄ Wind blowing across a glacier front picks up snow and ice crystals that are illuminated by the setting sun. Svalbard, Norway.

▲ A polar bear wanders across the sea ice under the rays of the midnight sun.

► By late spring, the sun illuminates the icy landscape through most of the night.

NEW LIFE ON THE ICE

D ays later we travel the frozen fjords of western Svalbard. Inside the fjords, the ice is flat and smooth. With binoculars I search the surface for seals and their pups. The newborn babies are quite helpless. They cannot withstand long periods of time in the freezing water, so they usually rest buried in snow lairs on the surface and wait for their mother's return. As I scan the fjord, I repeatedly lock onto little spots, questioning whether I am looking at a chunk of ice or a seal pup. This landscape is so huge and the air so clear that it is hard to get a sense of scale. As we travel farther into the fjord, it becomes obvious—little bundles of fur are scattered across the frozen fjord. This year the snow layer is so thin that the seal pups are left exposed on the ice. From the perspective of a polar bear, it is an all-you-can-catch buffet of tender seal.

A seal pup lies close to a breathing hole and waits for the return of its mother. She is busy keeping a number of breathing holes open, so that she has options if a polar bear is watching over one. For hours I have been lying on my stomach, inching closer to the pup. With my dark parka, I'm hoping I look like a seal. I started this photography session in the early evening, and it is now almost midnight. The temperature keeps dropping; it is close to -4 degrees Fahrenheit. I am starting to get tired and occasionally doze off.

Suddenly the urgent call of the baby seal grabs my attention. I hear a small splash. The mother must be at the bottom of the two-foot-deep hole in the ice. "*Juoeoeoeoeoe, juoeoeoeoe,*" I hear the seal pup yelping, encouraging the mother to come out and let it nurse. I hold completely still and don't even dare to take a picture as I watch the scene unfold. With the help of her side flippers, the mother climbs out of the hole. Cautiously, she observes her surroundings, then settles down and relaxes. The little pup quickly crawls over to her and

◄ A ringed seal pup waits for its mother to return from feeding. Svalbard, Norway.

begins to nurse. I just wait and observe, letting the mother get used to my presence. After a couple of minutes she disappears again.

I take the opportunity to crawl a bit closer. Just like the mother seal, I frequently lift my head and take a good look in all directions so that I am not suddenly surprised by a polar bear. I make sure my flare gun is loaded and the trigger is not frozen.

~

Hours later I am still lying on the ice. I have inched quite close to the hole by now, and I notice some activity. The pup begins to call, yet nothing happens. I am concentrating on the shot through my viewfinder when I hear *kchuak kchuak kchuak kchuak*. It sounds just like steps breaking through a thin layer of icy snow. I freeze. It cannot be my guide; I would have heard the snowmobile. A heat wave goes though my body. Could it be a polar bear sneaking up on me? I hardly dare to turn. My hand goes slowly to my flare gun and I begin to roll over, full of anticipation.

To my great surprise there is nothing for me to discover. I look from side to side, but I see nothing. I notice a black spot in the corner of my eye and turn, but it has already disappeared. Then I hear the sound again: *kchuak kchuak kchuak kchuak*. It begins to dawn on me. It is the mother seal scraping her strong claws on the ice to keep her other breathing hole open. I smile to myself and take a deep breath.

A moment later I hear the splashing again. The pup reacts with its calls. I quickly bring my wide-angle lens into position and frame the shot before the mother's head looks out of the water. I do not want to move at all when she appears. Through the lens I see the pup crawl closer to the hole. Then the mother appears. I hold off for a moment, then take the first image as she looks over to her pup. Warm, diffused light falls over the scene. The water on the mother's fur makes it shine and appear extremely soft. With great effort she pulls herself onto the ice. Her dark body shining in the morning sun reminds me of the polished soapstone figures of Inuit artists.

I am only a few feet from the mother and her pup. I hear her breathe and see her close her eyes while the little pup nurses and makes contented suckling noises. The hours on my belly on the frozen sea have been worth it as I am rewarded with a breathtaking scene. It seems as if I have become an invisible observer while the seals grant me a look into their lives. Soon the mother glides back into the water again. The baby has a lot of energy after drinking the milk, which is rich in fat. It rolls around in the snow, stretches itself, and tries out its own little claws.

My face feels frozen and my hands are numb, but I am so excited to be among the seals in this frozen world. Surrounded by the silent mountains, I let my eyes wander into the distance, where I see massive glacier walls towering over the ice on the fjord. It all seems frozen solid, yet the dynamic lines bear witness to the fact that the glacier is in constant motion. As if to affirm my thoughts, it sends a loud crack echoing down the valley.

◀ A mother ringed seal comes to her
breathing hole to check on her pup.

▲◀ Infant seal pups cannot withstand long periods of time in
the freezing water and must wait for their mothers on the ice.

▲◀ Ringed seal pups are born with pure white fur. Svalbard, Norway.
▲ A ringed seal mother nurses her pup. Svalbard, Norway.

◄◄ Thick-billed murres and pigeon guillemots congregate in sections of the Arctic Ocean that remain ice free through the winter. Svalbard, Norway.

► A pigeon guillemot lands on open water. Svalbard, Norway.

►► Following pages: Icebergs frozen into the ice of the Davis Strait begin to melt under the spring sun. Baffin Island, Canada. / A mother polar bear and her cubs rest on the sea ice.

INTO THE LIGHT

Spring is a short season in the Arctic. The sun climbs higher each day and stays longer above the horizon, soon erasing darkness from the Arctic altogether. The warming rays pour over the landscape until meltwater drips from icicles and cracks develop in the ocean ice. Through these cracks sunlight filters into the water, letting microscopic life begin to flourish, forming the basic and most important part of the food chain. Anything that is not white, such as gravel on a windblown ridge, a blade of grass, or a dark rock in a glacier wall, attracts the rays of the sun, bundles its energy, and then sends it off, melting the surrounding snow and ice. Over time, little creeks start to swell with meltwater, rushing into rivers and off to the sea.

Polar bear mothers have left their denning areas with their spring cubs in tow and now patrol the thinning ice, looking for seals. Millions of migrating birds hurry north to reach their nesting grounds. Flocks of eiders numbering in the thousands fly northward along the floe edge, spreading out along the Arctic Ocean. Geese and shorebirds follow. Their presence brings the tundra to life. Males of countless species announce their presence with beautiful calls and flashy courtship flights. No time is wasted; the birds lay their eggs just as the snow disappears. Nose down in a bouncy trot, half-white Arctic foxes zigzag their territory, hoping to flush a bird and steal its eggs. Their short barks echo across the tundra.

The caribou are well on their way north, heading for the Arctic plains to give birth to their young. Here the concentration of predators is lower, and the new vegetation is full of nutrients. What may appear to be a barren wasteland from a distance actually vibrates with life.

◄ Ice melts at the edge of Pond Inlet. Baffin Island, Canada.

◄◄ Fluke of a narwhal. Baffin Island, Canada.

► Thick-billed murres feed along the ice edge.

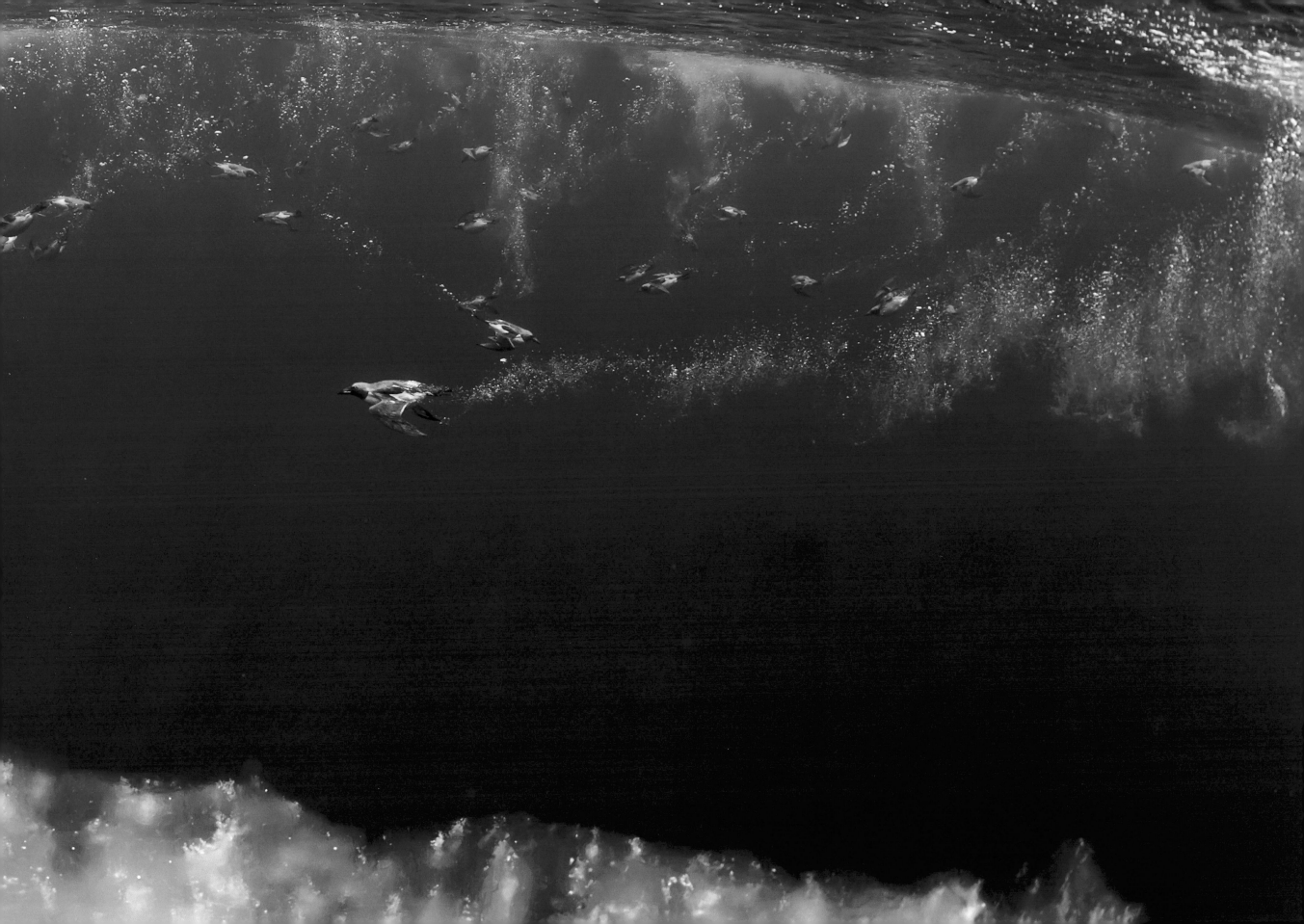

▲ A large male polar bear stands on his hind legs to investigate an area of broken sea ice. Baffin Bay, Canada.

▲ A king eider stops to rest on the ice during its spring migration. Baffin Island, Canada.

▲ King eiders during their spring migration on the east coast of Baffin Island, Canada.

◄ The wind and currents break sheets of ice and crush them together,

forming an ever-changing landscape of ice. Chukchi Sea.

▲ Ringed seals rest on the ice near a breathing and escape hole.

►► Kittiwakes gather in front of a glacier to feed. Svalbard, Norway.

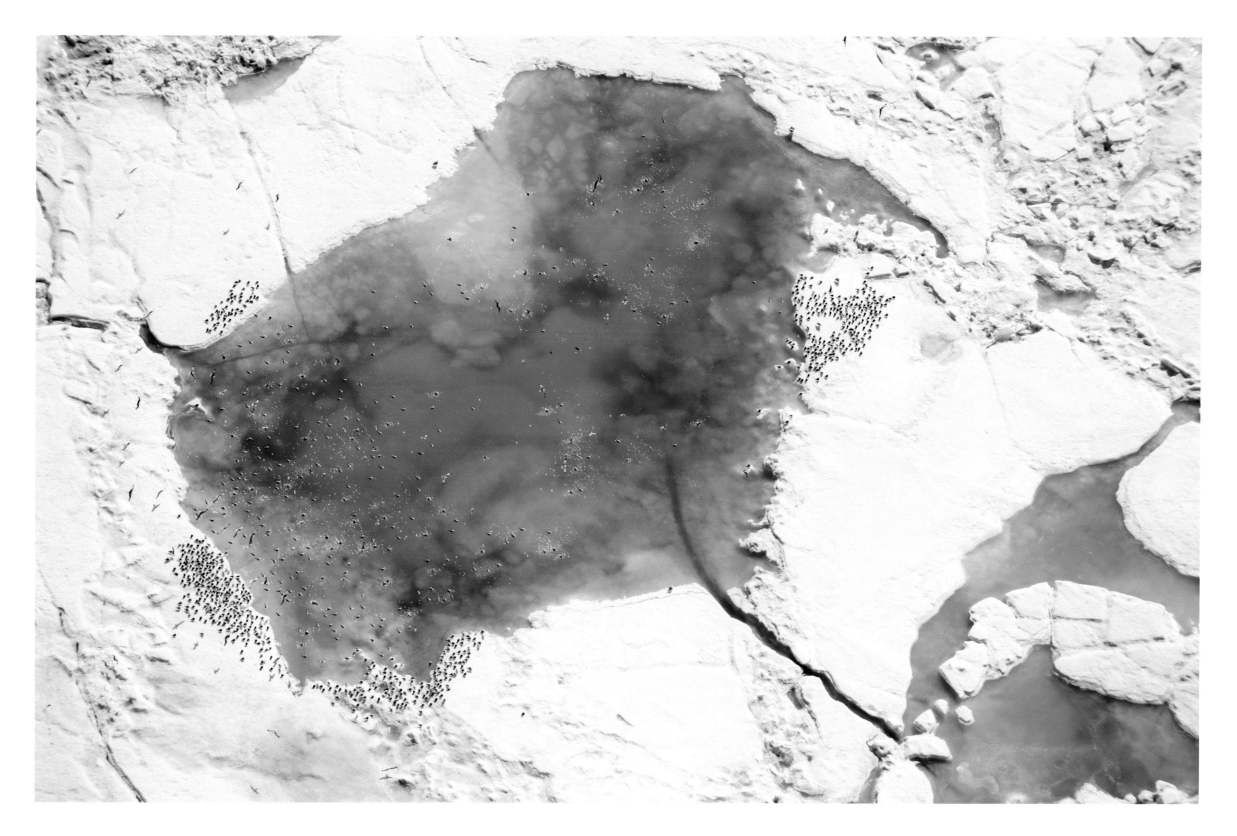

◄ Thick-billed murres rest on a pool of meltwater that has formed on top of the sea ice. Chukchi Sea, off the coast of Alaska.

▲ Kittiwakes gather near a pool of meltwater on the sea ice. Chukchi Sea.

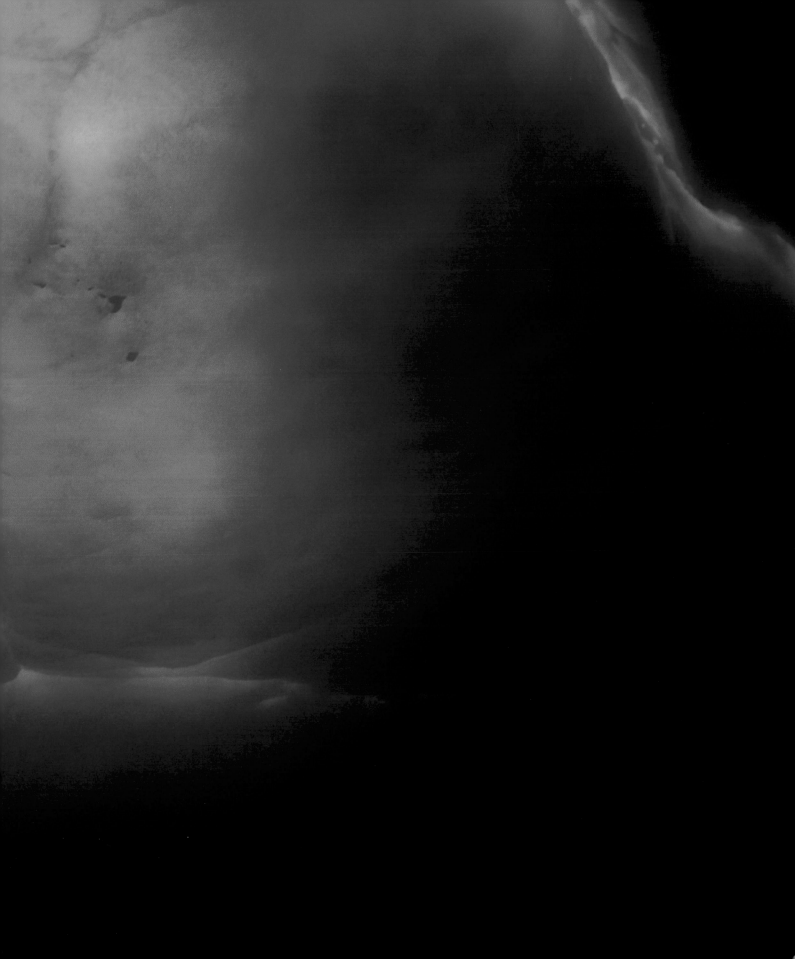

UNDER THE ICEBERGS

In order to truly know this place, I want to dive in the Arctic and photograph its underwater world. So, together with several Inupiat families and guides, I have traveled over one thousand miles across Baffin Island toward its northernmost point, pulling our gear behind us on traditional *qamutiqs*—practically indestructible Inupiat sleds.

Spring is on its way, but vast areas along the coast of the Arctic Ocean are still frozen. Near our camp, one crack at the edge of a massive iceberg has opened just enough for us to expand it with an ax so that a diver can slip through. In order to withstand the freezing water temperature, I am wearing a dry suit and a neoprene hood and gloves. The only area that is not covered is my face. Before I get in the water, I look up one last time and see the iceberg towering above me. I am eager to see what it will look like underneath. As I glide into the 30-degree water, the stinging cold takes my breath away. My exposed face feels instantly frozen, as if I have been shoved face first into a snowbank.

I sink slowly down and become aware of the landscape around me. From underneath, the iceberg has a completely different look. Floating like a spaceship in the dark ocean, the underwater side looks like an enormous sponge, while the fast ice that has formed around it is fairly smooth. Forty feet below the surface, I look up at this magnificent structure, which looks like some sort of futuristic architecture. When I lie on my back and look at the layer of fast ice above me, it shimmers like a transparent skin on the ocean, letting varying intensities of light shine through. Glowing, light-blue cracks vein the ice. Suddenly an Arctic jellyfish floats by, flashing colorful bioluminescent lights, just like a little spacecraft arriving at the mother ship. I almost forget to breathe as I marvel at the ingenuity of nature.

◄ An iceberg viewed from below the water with a layer of sea ice above. Baffin Island, Canada.

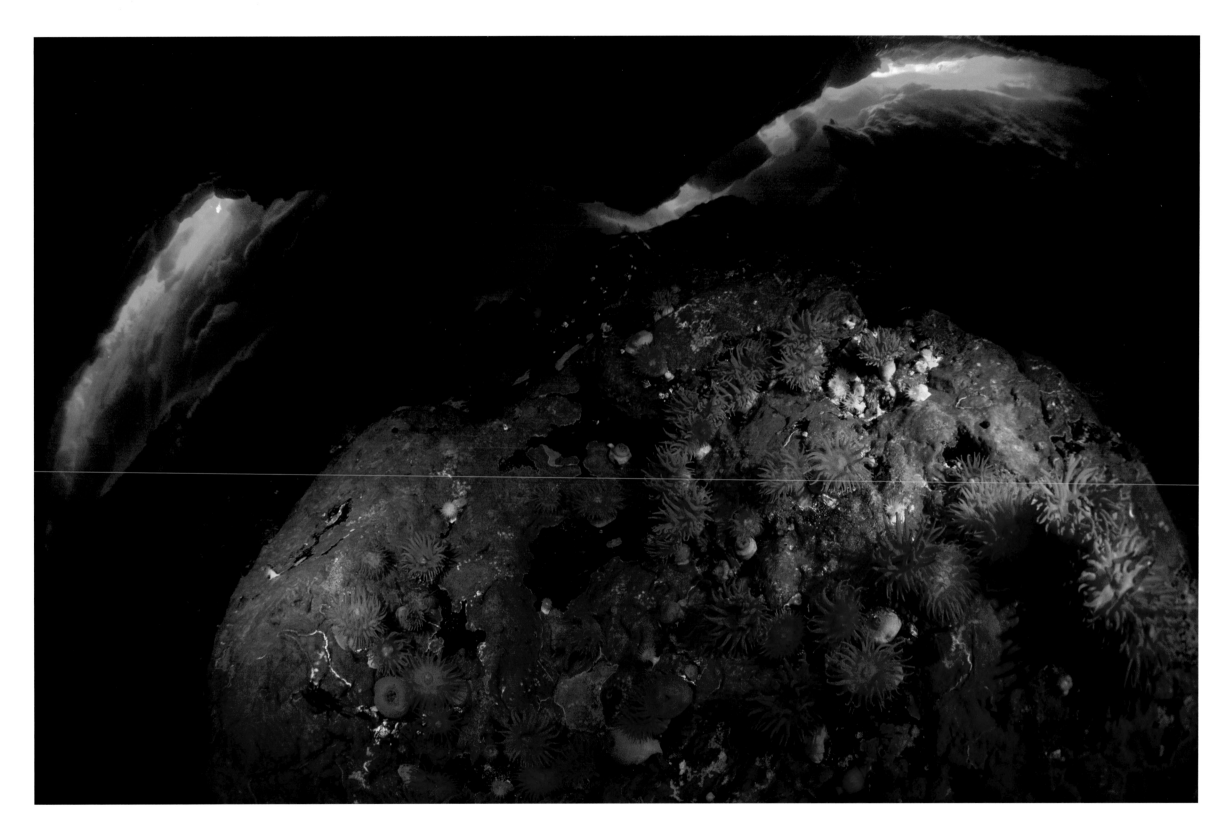

◄ Cracks allow seawater to escape to the surface of the ice where it collects in pools. Baffin Island, Canada.

▲ In a scene from the film, brilliant anemones flourish under the Arctic sea ice near Baffin Island, Canada. Courtesy MacGillivray Freeman Films.

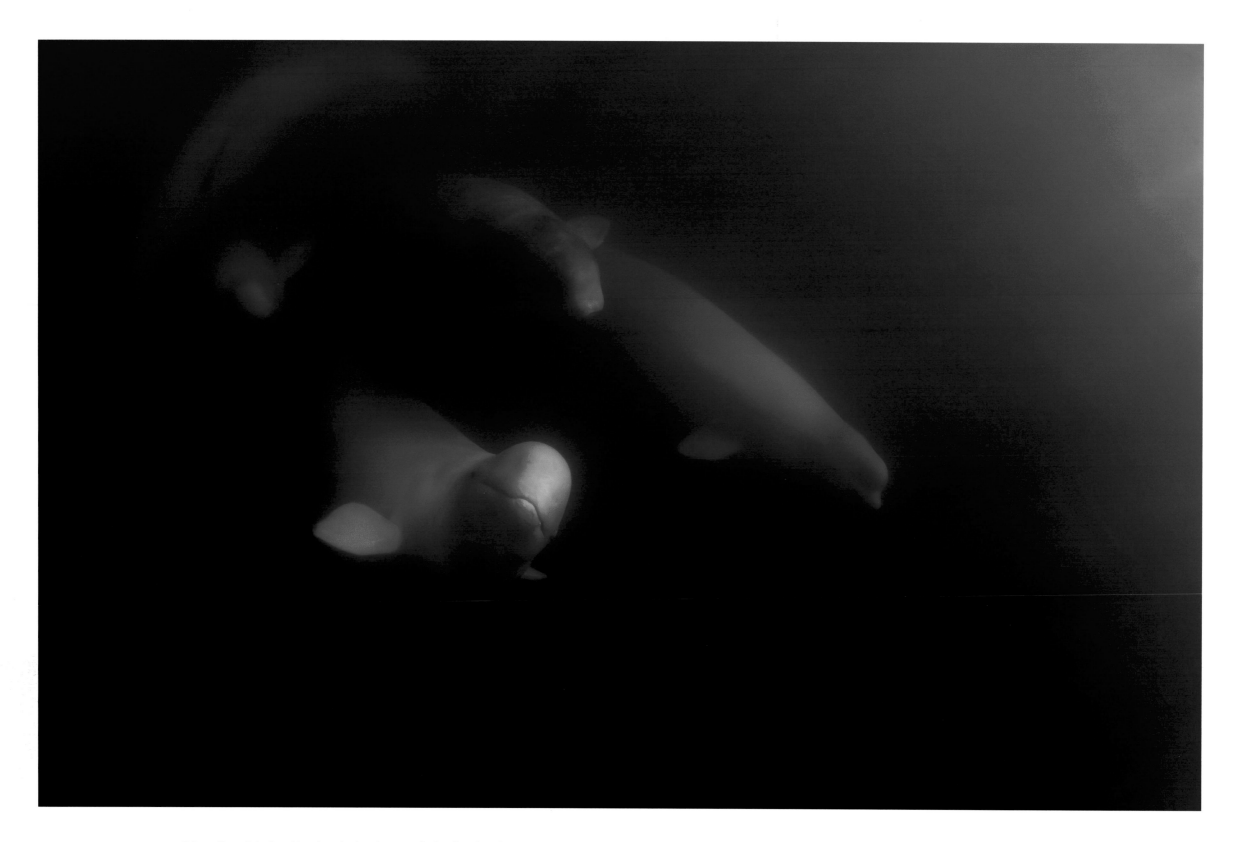

▲ Belugas live only in the cold arctic and subarctic waters. Hudson Bay, Canada.　　　　▶ Pieces of ice drifting in the Arctic Ocean off the coast of Baffin Island, Canada.

Breakup of the sea ice in the Arctic Ocean
off the coast of Point Hope, Alaska.

POLAR BEARS AT THE FIN WHALE CARCASS

It is the end of spring in Svalbard. The MacGillivray Freeman film team has joined us on a sailboat heading north along the western edge of the archipelago, hoping to reach a small bay in the northwestern corner—Holmiabukta, where a dead fin whale washed up the previous year and fed many polar bears throughout the summer. We have heard rumors that the carcass might still be around and could attract some bears.

The next day we arrive at the mouth of Holmiabukta Bay. We need to await high tide so we can slip over the shallow entrance. A beautiful glacier greets us from the far end. Half of the bay is still covered with a shallow layer of ice, giving us just enough space to anchor in the center. At first glance, no bears come into view and we don't see the whale carcass. I wonder if the winter ice might have moved the carcass away from shore, leaving it on the sea floor. But as the tide goes down, the first bones of the enormous spine of the fin whale appear. And it does not take long before our guide, Audun, discovers a female polar bear resting with her cub beside a large boulder on the far shore. She is lying lazily on her stomach, with her cub nestled beside her, looking quite like a cream-colored boulder herself. The bear knows not to waste any energy and is simply waiting for the tide to go down far enough so she can reach the whale meat that remains on the carcass.

The tide keeps dropping and suddenly hits the magic mark. I watch the polar bear stand up and turn to face downhill. As if she were a seal, she gives herself just enough of a push to slide down the snowbank on her stomach, her cub right behind her. At the

◄ A first-year polar bear cub waits on a boulder as its mother dives down to the remaining meat on a fin whale carcass in Holmiabukta Bay. Svalbard, Norway.

bottom she gets up and strolls to the carcass, elegantly walking over the spine that has been picked completely clean by many polar bear mouths. She is now on the alert, constantly probing the air with her nose and looking around. Then she enters the water through a small opening in the ice that has formed around the carcass. The remaining meat must be just below the surface, and she knows to dive for it. The little cub is reluctant to follow and watches from shore.

In the polar bear world, the females not only carry the burden of raising the offspring alone, but need to watch out for hungry male bears, which have been known to kill cubs. Suddenly, a large male polar bear appears and heads down the hill. The mother bear is preoccupied with diving for the meat and does not see him, but the tiny cub does and starts to complain. It struggles over the whale spine to get closer to its mother as the male arrives at the shoreline. When the mother surfaces again, she hears the desperate cub. Her instinct tells her to fight. Like an arrow, she shoots out of the water and leaps across the backbone of the whale, attacking the male bear with a deep roar and a wide-open mouth that exposes her massive teeth. The male, twice her size, confronts her with the same open jaws. The roaring grows even more intense, but to my surprise the male takes a step backward and then continues to retreat. The female stands her ground until he

turns, walks a little distance away, and lies down. She has proven her point and has the whale carcass to herself for a while longer.

It is well past midnight when fog moves in, turning the landscape bluish gray and swallowing all other colors. The bears soon disappear in the mist. Exhausted, I climb into my tiny bunk to catch up on sleep.

When I get up a few hours later and emerge onto the deck, an incredible sight greets me. The sun is just breaking through the fog, revealing a scene I had not even dared to dream about. More than ten polar bears, including cubs, have gathered around the carcass. The tide is even lower and two females with their cubs are standing on the whale's backbone, while another bear's head is poking out of a hole in the ice just in front of the skeleton. The other bears are lying close by, watching the feeding intently.

~

We have been at Holmiabukta for a week and have watched the number of bears at the carcass grow to more than twenty and then drop again. After spending day after day observing, filming, and photographing, we now recognize individual bears and can pick out new arrivals. Some of the newcomers arriving from the sea ice have beautiful white fur, while the fur of the bears that have been at the

carcass for a long time is yellowish from the whale oil in the water.

I am beginning to wonder if this carcass is a blessing or a curse for the bears. It attracts large numbers of them, but it hardly seems to provide enough meat to feed them well. The cubs of the bears that have been around for a while appear malnourished and far too small for the end of June. With so many bears close to the carcass, a lot of energy is spent fighting over the food. At the same time, the meat is a sure bet for the bears, which are now stranded on land as the ice retreats. In spring and summer, without access to seals, polar bears have to live on scraps, mainly surviving on the valuable fat reserves they have built up during winter. Stuck on land, polar bears fast until sea ice freezes in the fall. They will eat bird eggs and a variety of other things, but do not materially benefit from these meager pickings. Polar bears are in their true element when hunting seals out on the ice, which in my mind is why the newly arriving bears look so much healthier. They are so specialized to hunt on the surface of the sea ice, they are unlikely to persist in an ice-free Arctic. It is ironic that the polar bear, the king of the Arctic, which has always been able to withstand anything nature throws its way—the most severe cold, the fiercest storms, and the coldest water—now faces a new enemy it is not equipped for: global warming.

◄ The little meat that remains on a whale carcass sparks fierce competition among the polar bears that have gathered to feed. Svalbard, Norway.

▲◄ A mother and her cub wait for their turn at the whale carcass.

▲ Whale oil in the water tints the bears' fur yellow. Svalbard, Norway.

▲ A polar bear cub plays on the ice. Barents Sea.

◄ A polar bear dives down to a fin whale carcass to tear the remaining scraps of meat from the bones. Svalbard, Norway.

▲ Returning from the remains of the whale carcass, a polar bear comes up for air through the disintegrating layer of ice.

► A large number of polar bears travel to the fin whale carcass in the summer,

when melting sea ice makes it difficult to hunt for seals. Svalbard, Norway.

◄ A mother polar bear and her two-year-old cubs eye the whale carcass from a distance while other bears are present. Svalbard, Norway.

◄ The mother and her cubs cautiously wait for their turn to feed.

▲ Two males, above, circle each other at the whale carcass on a foggy morning. Svalbard, Norway.

▶ A first-year cub follows its mother along the
shore of Holmiabukta Bay. Svalbard, Norway.

▲ A narwhal dives deep into the ice-covered fjord in search of Arctic cod. Baffin Island, Canada.

▲ A narwhal shows its fluke as it dives. Narwhals often spend twenty minutes under water before surfacing for air. Baffin Island, Canada.

◄ Seals enjoy the warming rays of the sun as they rest before diving below the melting ice. Beaufort Sea, Alaska.

▲ A ringed seal rests near a breathing hole in the Beaufort Sea, Alaska.

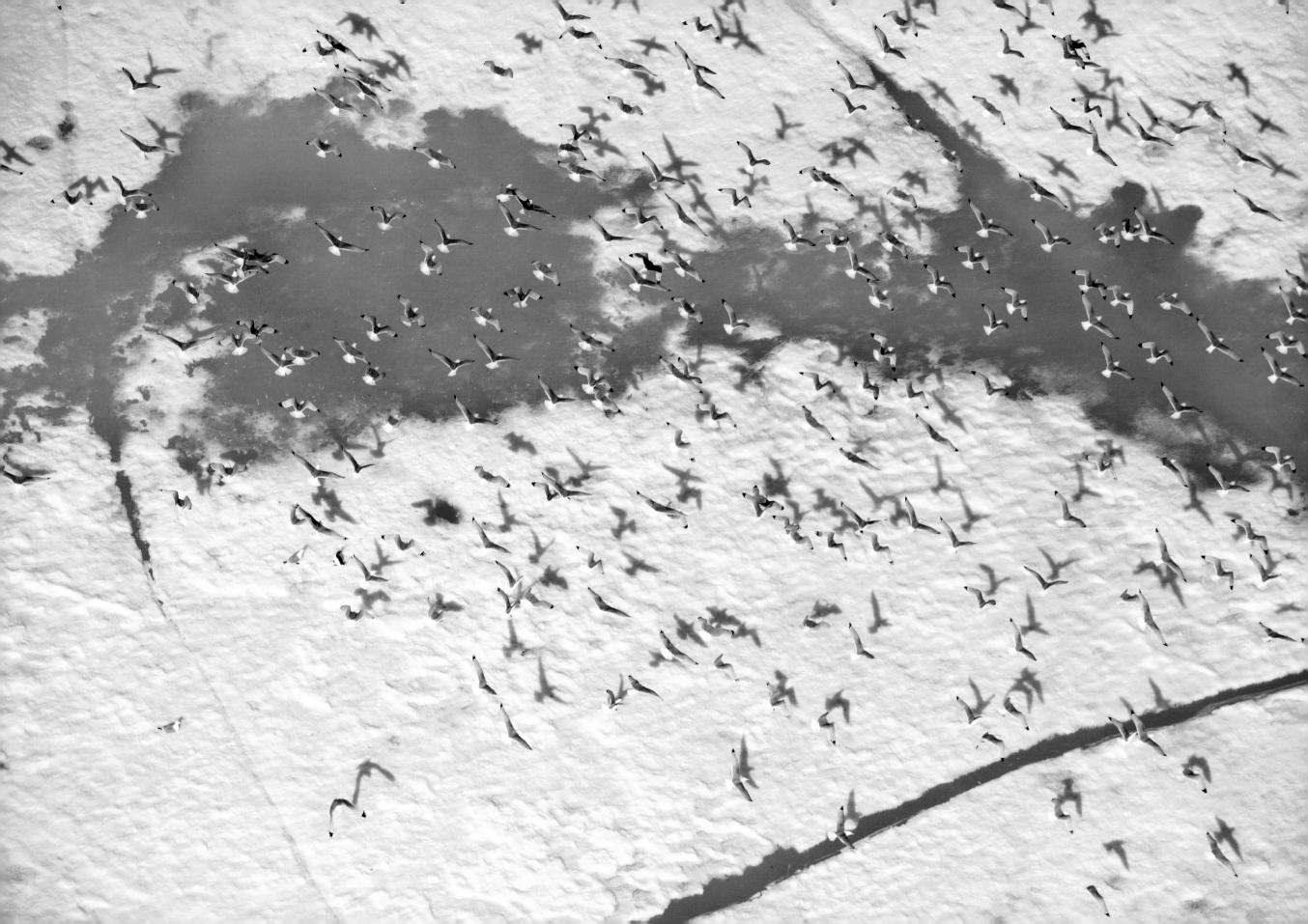

◀ Kittiwakes fly over the ice of the Chukchi Sea, Alaska.

▲ Ringed seals lie on the sea ice near their breathing holes. Beaufort Sea, Alaska.

▲ The Western Arctic caribou herd migrates along the coast of the Arctic Ocean each spring. Arctic National Wildlife Refuge, Alaska.

▶ Caribou are well adapted to travel across mountainous terrain. North Slope, Alaska.

CARIBOU

We hurriedly unload several weeks' worth of gear off the bush plane. The pilot bids us a quick good-bye and the plane races off, leaving us in a cloud of dust. My wife, Emil, and I are standing alone in the Utukok uplands in the northwestern corner of Alaska. This is one of the most remote regions in North America— some 460 miles from Fairbanks, Alaska's northernmost city. We are here in hopes of finally documenting the most impressive wildlife migration left on the North American continent. Every year, 400,000 to 500,000 caribou from the Western Arctic herd migrate from their winter range on the Seward Peninsula, across the Brooks Range, into the National Petroleum Reserve for the spring calving. Totaling some two thousand miles, it is the longest migration of any land mammal. We have tried several times in past years, without success, to find the caribou. One might assume that finding such a huge number of animals would be an easy task, but caribou are unpredictable and can simply disappear in the vast Arctic landscape. There is an old Native saying: "No one knows the ways of the wind and the caribou." We certainly have learned this lesson.

~

In our tent on the riverbank, caribou are on my mind as the soft rippling of the water lulls me to sleep. In a dream I see them migrating across the tundra. But something is wrong. The sound of the river has grown to a roar. Thinking that a wave of meltwater from the mountains is about to burst through the tent, I awaken with a rush of adrenaline and rip open the tent door. Then I understand. "The caribou have arrived!" I shout to waken Emil. Hundreds of them are rushing into the river. The water splashes and foams. As they climb out on our side and move

(to page 115)

▶ Hundreds of thousands of caribou travel to the coast of the Arctic Ocean, where a cooling summer breeze provides relief from mosquitoes. Canning River Delta, Alaska.

(from page 110)

on, their hooves clatter on the rocks and their strange calls fill the air.

Emil and I scramble up a nearby ridge, where we can see for miles in all directions. Only now do I begin to understand the scope of the arriving herd. The rolling hills toward the east are filled with caribou as far as we can see. Bands of animals flow over the tundra and blanket the plains. Through my binoculars I see little brown dots bouncing across the tussocked tundra alongside the cows. These are the newborn calves, which follow the herd only hours after their birth. It is hard to express the joy that overcomes me; I have waited for this moment for years. For me, these caribou represent true wilderness. In the vastness of the Arctic, they follow their ancient rhythm over the course of the seasons, just as they always have.

Now a large band of caribou reaches the sandbank on the other side of the river. They are reluctant to enter the rushing water. With ever more animals arriving, their restlessness grows until a few make a run for the river and the herd instinct takes over. It is close to midnight. As fog starts to creep up the river valley, I decide to go down to the river to be right there among the caribou when the warm rays of the morning sun break through the fog. At the river's edge I lie down in a shallow depression and pull a camouflage blanket over myself. From my hiding spot I get a close look at the drama that is unfolding. I see how the river current grabs the caribou and pushes them downstream. Mothers place themselves upstream to create an eddy for their calves, but sometimes the current still gets hold of them. Calves baa and their mothers answer with coughlike barks and grunts. The calling becomes intense, and I can feel the fear and desperation as the young get carried away. Chaos breaks out. As many single calves climb out of the river, the waiting mothers try to detect their young by smell, while confused calves try to pair up with any cow. If they do not find the right mother, however, they may be kicked away. It is hard to watch, but I remind myself that this is part of nature.

~

We have not slept in almost thirty hours, and exhaustion is catching up with us. As we stumble back over the tundra toward camp, we spot a lone caribou calf just ahead. I quickly drop to my knees so I don't scare it, and Emil does the same. Surprisingly, the calf heads straight toward us. Emil rises slowly to her feet and, without fear, the calf walks directly to her. It presses its soft little snout directly into Emil's down vest, as if wanting to nurse. I see Emil's eyes fill with tears. When the calf wanders on across the tundra, we breathe again.

We can't help but feel saddened by the vulnerability of these small creatures and the precariousness of their existence.

As I set up the stove back at camp, Emil goes to do some sound recording without the clicking of my camera. I look up to see her running toward me. "I found a caribou calf trapped in a hole!" Emil gasps. "We need to rescue it!" Her eyes are full of hope and determination. I share her emotions, but what are we going to do? We can't raise this calf on powdered milk! But as if she has read my mind, Emil goes on, "There's a single cow on the other side of the willows. She's pacing and calling. I think this could be her calf."

A few moments later I stand over the little calf, which is huddled, exhausted, at the bottom of the hole. I grab Emil's raincoat, wrap it around the calf, and put the whole bundle into Emil's arms. The calf fidgets for a moment, but Emil pulls it gently to her and it calms down.

I stand back as Emil slowly moves in the direction of the agitated mother. She puts the calf down and backs away. To our great surprise, the little calf first follows Emil. But then a loud call from the cow catches the calf's attention, and it runs straight to her. We are overwhelmed with joy as we watch them touch noses and then see the calf suckle for a few moments. As we watch them turn and follow the herd, Emil's eyes fill with tears again. But this time, they are tears of joy.

◄◄ Caribou cross the Utukok River during their annual spring migration.

◄ Caribou climb the banks of the Utukok River. National Petroleum Reserve, Alaska.

▲ Just days after birth, calves follow their mothers on the long migration, even swimming across wide rivers.

▲ Young caribou calves depend on their mothers for survival and must stay close during the migration.

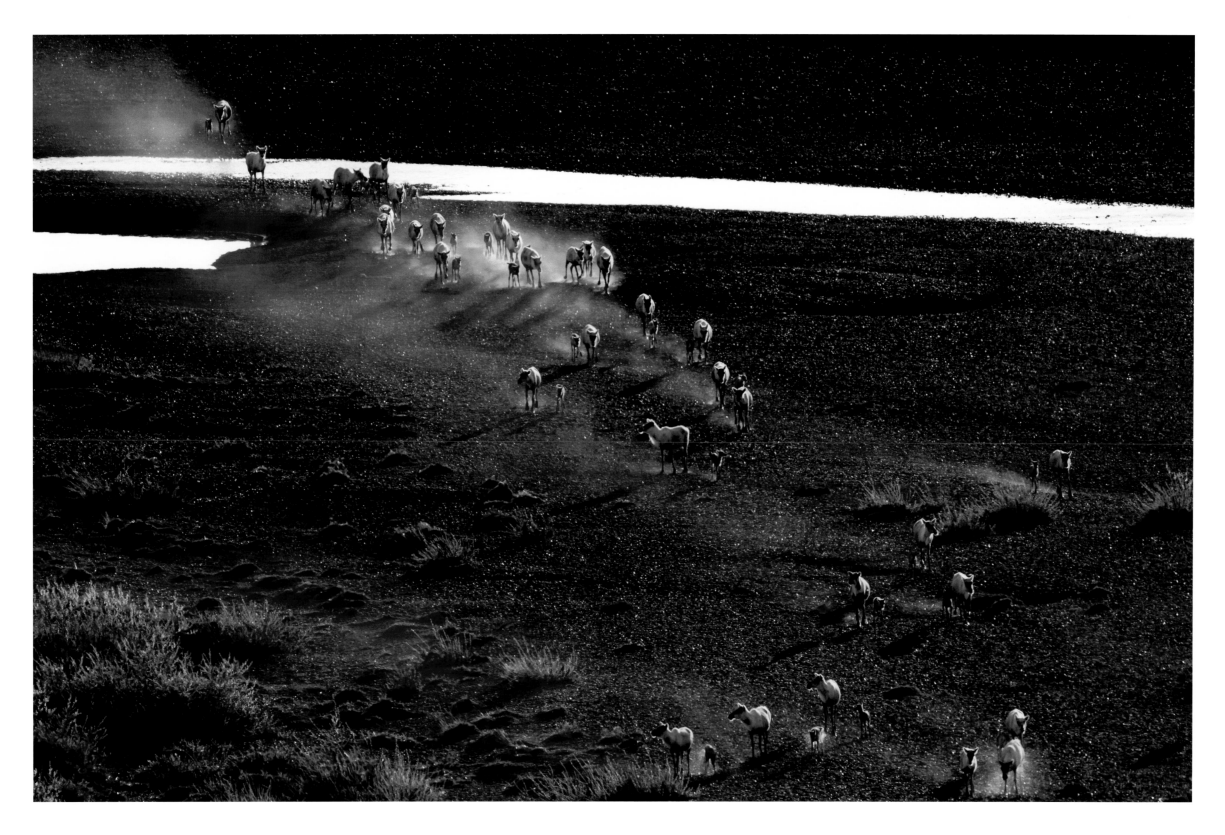

◄ With a trek of about two thousand miles, the migration of the Western Arctic caribou herd is the longest of any land mammal.

▲ Caribou travel west across the bed of the Utukok River in the National Petroleum Reserve. Northwest Alaska.

▲ In a herd of tens of thousands, a caribou calf calls to keep close track of its mother.

► Each year the Western Arctic caribou herd travels between its winter range on the Seward Peninsula across the Brooks Range into the National Petroleum Reserve for the spring calving.

◀◀ A grizzly mother and her three cubs move through the Arctic National Wildlife Refuge following the Porcupine caribou herd.

▲ Grizzly bears follow the migrating caribou, preying on animals that are injured or sick, or calves that are vulnerable or die during river crossings. National Petroleum Reserve, Alaska

►► Following pages: At the end of June, large herds begin to gather on the coastal plains north of the Brooks Range. The tundra turns green and gold in the warmer temperatures, but the caribou also face thick swarms of mosquitoes. Arctic National Wildlife Refuge, Alaska. / After her eggs hatch, a female snowy owl protects her fragile chicks from the harsh environment. Near Barrow, Alaska.

SUMMER

WARMTH AND RENEWAL

Under the never-setting sun, life explodes as bird calls fill the air across the tundra. Eggs hatch and parents are kept busy feeding their chicks. It is the time of plenty, but nature seems to know that summer will not last. The chicks need to grow up and be able to fly soon.

Melting snow and ice cannot drain through the permafrost, and the water forms shallow ponds. This abundance of wetlands is the ideal habitat for the shorebirds, geese, ducks, and loons. But the wet environment attracts another group of winged creatures—mosquitoes. Their swarms drive hundreds of thousands of caribou closer to the Arctic Ocean and into the mountains, where steady breezes provide a bit of relief from the plague. Yet, even as they are a nuisance to mammals, mosquitoes are an important food source for birds.

As summer progresses, the ocean becomes increasingly ice free. Thick, multiyear ice remains, but it is far from shore. This is the only ice that lasts through the summer, until freeze-up occurs again in fall. Walruses haul out on such ice, allowing them to remain over the clam beds they rely upon. For as long as possible, polar bears hang on to the annual ice that melts each summer, using it as a platform to hunt for seals. But soon the time comes when the bears need to head for land. As winds and currents push the remaining ice sheets around, the bears can end up hundreds of miles from shore. While most animals thrive during summer, polar bears find that life gets harder. Once they are back on land, they have to survive without seals—their most nutritious food. And the sooner the ice melts, the longer this season grows for the bears.

◄ ◄ Preceding pages: Porcupine caribou cross the Hulahula River. They are named for the Porcupine River that runs throughout most of their range. / The Hulahula River cuts through the Brooks Range, flowing north to the Arctic Ocean. Arctic National Wildlife Refuge, Alaska.

▲ Thousands of Porcupine caribou migrate south along the bed of the Hulahula River. Arctic National Wildlife Refuge, Alaska.

▲ A grizzly bear surveys its surroundings along the Canning River. Arctic National Wildlife Refuge, Alaska.   ▶ Members of the Western Arctic caribou herd cross the Kukpuk River in northwestern Alaska.

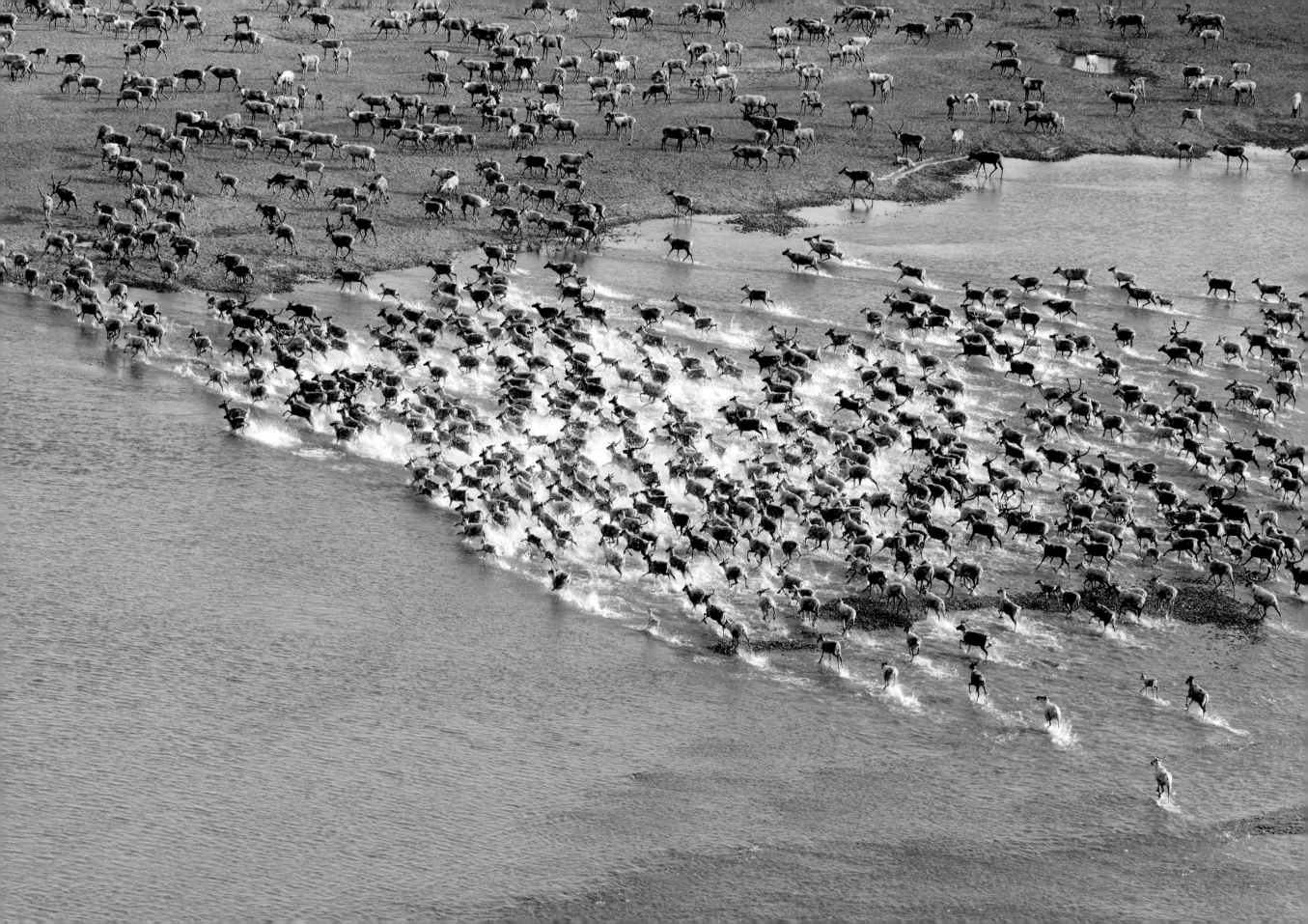

◄ Members of the Central Arctic caribou herd migrate across the Canning River Delta at the border of the Arctic National Wildlife Refuge, Alaska.   ▲ With more than 350,000 members, the Western Arctic herd is Alaska's biggest caribou herd. Western Arctic, Alaska.

THE SNOWY OWL

Everything is prepared: my camera pack on my back, a camouflaged blind under one arm, and my sleeping bag and mat under the other. I want to set up a blind to photograph a pair of snowy owls and their freshly hatched chicks, and must be as swift as possible because owls can be very protective of their nests.

With its pure white feathered robe and wide, powerful wings, the snowy owl is without question one of the most beautiful birds of the Arctic. In the far northern tip of Alaska, snowy owls find an ideal habitat for nesting and raising their young. It is a fairly flat landscape, consisting of many ponds and lakes surrounded by wet tundra. Snowy owls carefully choose little elevated islands in this wet tundra to scratch out their nests. In years when there is plenty of prey because the lemming population explodes, a snowy owl may see several of its neighbors' nests, marked with the white dots of females, loosely scattered across the tundra.

As I get closer to the nest, the female comes down like a fury from heaven, talons outstretched. Hunched over, with the owl in the sky above me, I move forward. The bird circles and calls. The next moment I feel its talons hit my back. Some thirty yards from the nest, I drop all my gear and pull the camouflaged tent out of its bag. It automatically unfolds and I jump inside. A few moments later the commotion is over and the female returns to the nest. After a quick check that everything is in order, she turns over the last remaining egg and puffs up her feathers while rocking back and forth to nestle her chicks between her plumes. She slowly closes her eyes and goes to sleep.

The first hours pass and nothing happens. The female simply dozes, occasionally glancing at her surroundings. The male is sitting

◄ A snowy owl sits on its remaining clutch while warming one chick that has already hatched. National Petroleum Reserve, Alaska.

on a slightly elevated spot some two hundred yards to the west. In contrast to the female, he seems alert. He needs to provide the female and chicks with a constant supply of food. Like a radar antenna, his head turns effortlessly 180 degrees. When he locks onto a lemming, he rocks his head left to right for increased depth perception, then quickly lifts up into the air and glides over the tundra, as silent as a shadow. Lightning fast, he drops down on his prey with razor-sharp talons.

I quickly move back to the tent window, where I can observe the nest. I want to see how the male delivers the food to the female. She has already realized that he has hunted sucessfully. In anticipation, she starts a yearning call, watching his every move. With strong, elegant strokes he approaches the nest, but lands a few feet from the knoll. Now the female calls even louder. I look through the viewfinder and see both birds, but the male is half cut off in the frame. His piercing yellow eyes look in all directions as he walks toward the female, so I don't dare move the lens, not even an inch. After a few seconds, the male disappears again, leaving the lemming behind. The female carefully dissects the little rodent and feeds tiny pieces of flesh to the chicks that appear beneath her feathers. It does not take

long until every bit is consumed and the female goes back to sleep. I, too, am getting tired, and I roll myself up in my sleeping bag.

Even as I doze, my ears seem to register what is going on around me. I hear the alarm calls of the mother and quickly get to my knees to peer out of the tent. I recognize a long-tailed jaeger as it dives down from the sky right at the female. At the last moment it pulls up into the air again, gains some height, then approaches once more. It seems to enjoy harassing the owl, knowing that she does not dare fly up and leave her chicks exposed. The jaeger becomes bolder, but eventually the female owl has had enough and springs up suddenly, throwing her talons toward the sky and barely missing the intruder. The jaeger gets the message and flies on.

∼

Forty-eight hours later I am still in the same spot and not too much has changed, though I am more familiar with the games of the harassing jaeger and can anticipate the return of the male by listening to the female's calls. The last egg has finally hatched, and a puffy white chick has joined the owl family. A low fog lingers, but

every now and again I see sunlight flood across the tundra in waves. Suddenly the wind stops. This fills me with hope because the wind has been carrying the ocean fog inland. Above I can see blue sky, and in the distance I see the warm sunlight slowly approaching. This might be the night for the shots I have envisioned.

The male has not brought food to the nest in a while. I look around to see where he is perched. As I spot him behind my tent, he suddenly flies up into the air. At that moment, the midnight sun breaks through the fog and paints its warm orange colors on the owl's wings, as if they were a white canvas. I follow his flight and see him bounce onto the tundra. With a lemming in his talons, the male flies for the nest. My hand is trembling with excitement, ready to release the shutter the instant the male enters the frame. I leave both eyes open, one looking through the lens, the other watching the scene. *Click, click, click, click, click*—a rapid burst from my camera and I capture the moment in golden light. I almost don't dare to breathe as I review the images. But there it is—the photograph I was hoping for: the male in his full glory with his wings wide open, and the female calling for him.

◂ A female snowy owl's feathers are flecked with brown; the male's are pure white.

▲ When a jaeger attacks, the female snowy owl jumps into the air to protect her young.

▲ Snowy owl chick.

▲ A male snowy owl arrives at the nest. National Petroleum Reserve, Alaska.

◄ One snowy owl chick is already much bigger and more active than its siblings that hatched days later.

▶ The male must constantly provide food to help the chicks grow quickly during the short summer season. National Petroleum Reserve, Alaska.

▲ A male golden plover incubates its eggs while the female stands guard. Ivvavik National Park, Canada.

► Sunset to the north on the upper Firth River. Ivvavik National Park, Canada.

◄ Innissiaq Hill on the coastal plains of the Firth River. Ivvavik National Park, Canada.

▲ A peregrine falcon nests along the cliffs of the Utukok River. National Petroleum Reserve, Alaska.

► A whimbrel in its summer nesting grounds near Hudson Bay, Canada.

► Reflection Pond in the Firth River Valley. Ivvavik National Park, Canada.

◄ In the early summer, groups of up to a thousand beluga whales have been known to congregate in the water south of Kasegaluk Lagoon. National Petroleum Reserve, Alaska.

▲ Kasegaluk Lagoon is one of the largest lagoon systems in the Arctic, running many miles along the coast of the Chukchi Sea.

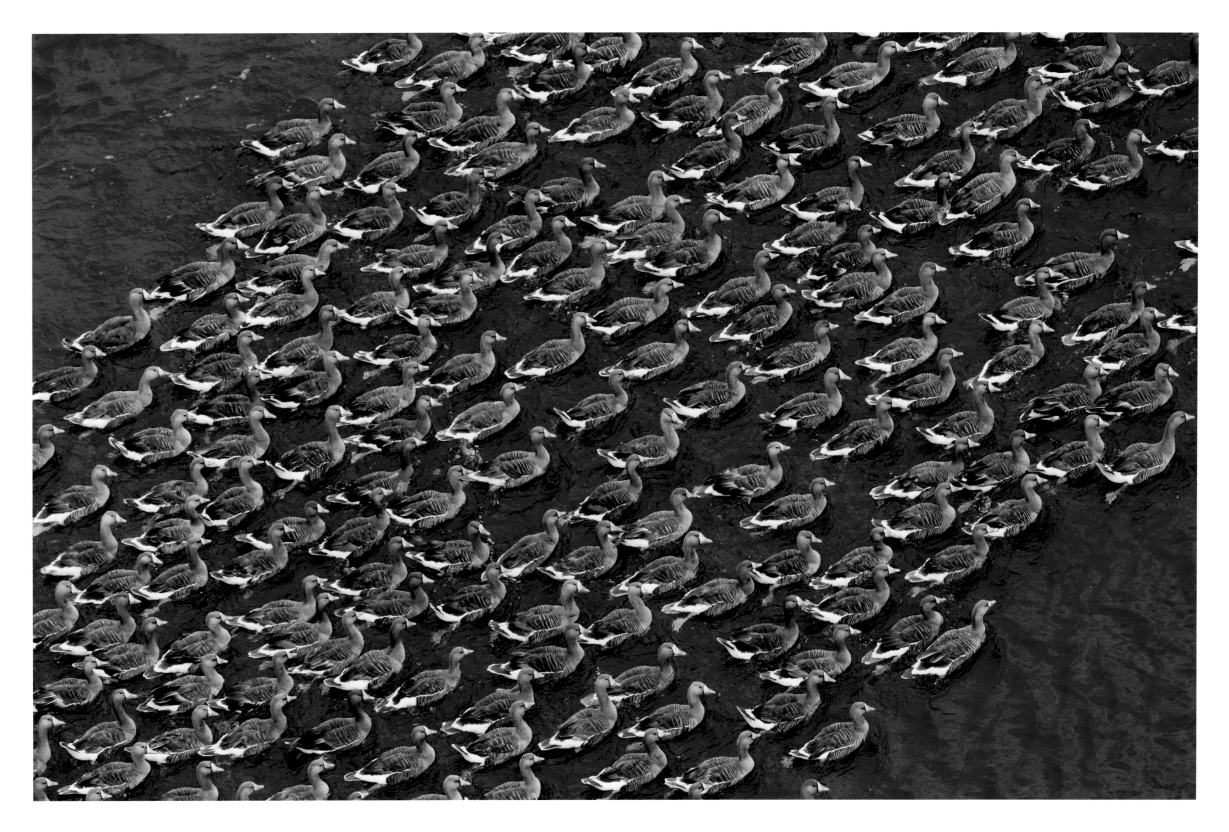

◄ A wetland habitat near Teshekpuk Lake, Alaska.

▲ A large group of white-fronted geese near Teshekpuk Lake.

▲ A newly hatched chick emerges from the protective feathers of its mother while she incubates her remaining eggs. Beaufort Sea, Canada.

▶ An arctic tern nests on a barrier island along the Yukon Coast. Beaufort Sea, Canada.

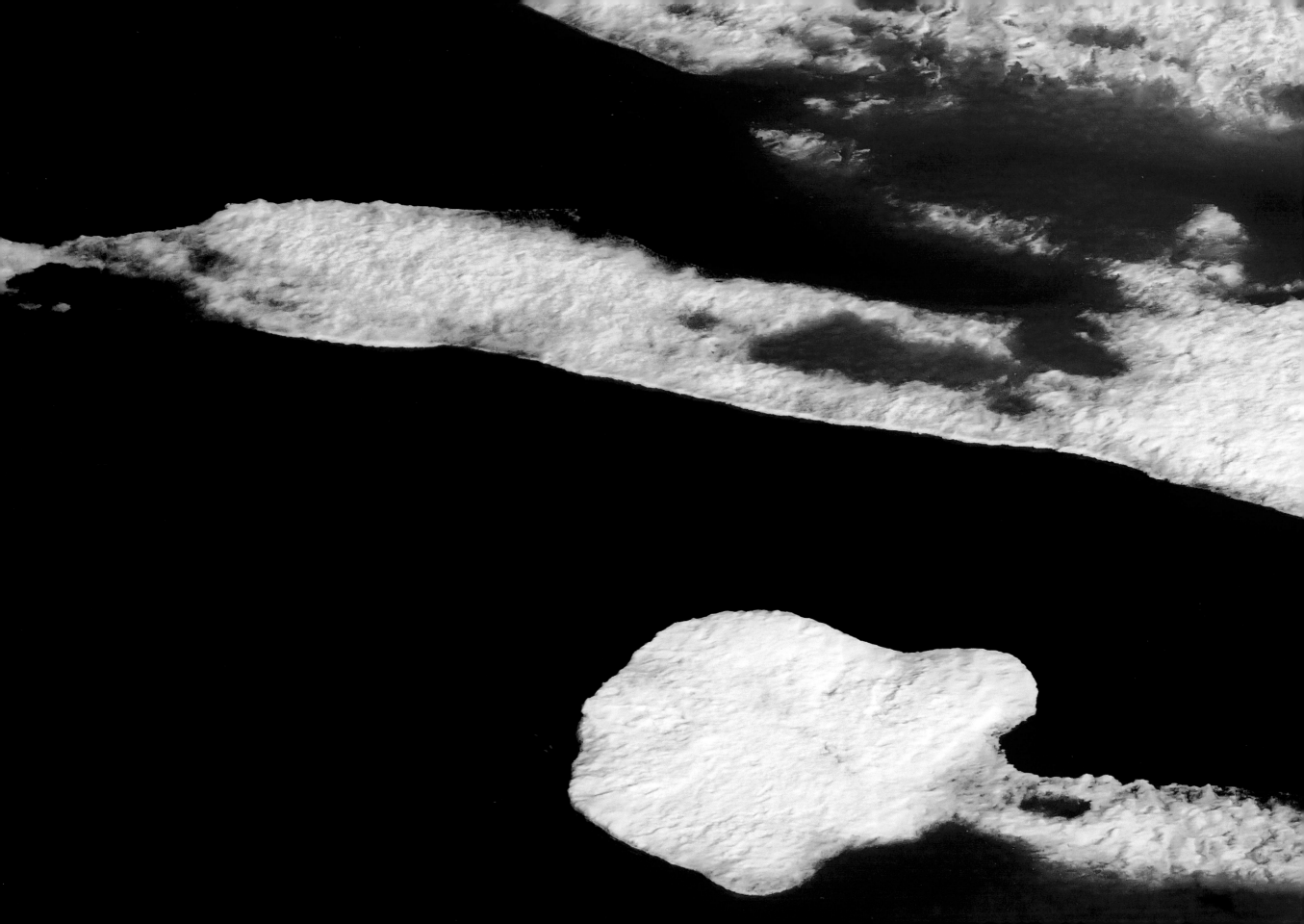

▲ Polar bear cubs are often born in pairs. Svalbard, Norway.

▲ A polar bear cub inspects its own reflection at the edge of an ice floe. Barents Sea, Norway.

◄ While nursing her young cubs, a mother polar bear seems to fall into a meditative state.

▲ Ocean swells rock an ice floe where a mother polar bear and her cubs rest. Barents Sea, Norway.

▲ A mother polar bear assesses the threat posed by an approaching male.

▶ Ears flattened in fear, the mother polar bear and her cubs jump between ice floes to make their escape. Barents Sea, Norway.

▲ A mother polar bear probes the air for seals or other bears. Barents Sea.

▶ Polar bear cubs reaffirm the bond with their mothers by touching noses. Barents Sea, Norway.

(from page 156)

begins digging in the ice while the other seems to be fascinated with his own reflection. In my mind's eye I see the cub leaning over the edge of the ice, looking straight down into the water as if staring into his own eyes.

~

One particular night we watch a male polar bear slowly working his way toward our female. The female is resting close to our boat after feeding on a seal and nursing the cubs. It is a tough job being a mother polar bear on the pack ice. She gets little sleep because she always needs to be alert to threats from marauding males, and she has endless demands from playful and hungry cubs. Exhaustion has finally overtaken our female, and she is sleeping. Her cubs play while the male quietly approaches, often swimming between the ice floes. With only his head above water, he disappears from view down at water level.

The crew has grown attached to the mother and cubs, and those of us awake on deck intently watch the scene unfold. The male, not knowing exactly where the female is, climbs out onto the ice just as she wakes up to check her surroundings. She quickly detects him and huffs over to her cubs to grab their attention. Intense seconds follow. As the female assesses the intruder, he quickly slips back into the water and continues toward her. She gives the cubs a sign and they all bolt, ears pinned back, running for their lives, jumping from ice floe to ice floe and swimming when the distance between the floes is too great. Sometime the cubs cling to their mother's back for a moment, but they can't hang on for long. The whole scene seems frantic, and we feel as if we can sense their fear. They keep going long after they make good their escape.

This event, and the entire week we spend observing these bears, leaves me in awe of a polar bear mother's dedication to her cubs. It is incredible to witness her gentleness and her fierce protectiveness as she teaches them the skills they will need when the time comes to fend for themselves. The images in my memory are as vivid to me as those I capture with my camera, and as indelible.

The male polar bear approaches as the mother and cubs flee. Barents Sea, Norway.

◄ A mother polar bear and her cub travel across loose pack ice on the eastern shore of Nordaustlandet. Svalbard, Norway.

▲ A walrus surfaces for air after a long dive. Barents Sea, Norway.

◄ A polar bear moves across the ice floes of the broken-up sea ice and among
large glacier icebergs from the Austfonna ice cap. Barents Sea, Norway.

▲ Polar bears have a thick layer of fat that helps them stay afloat in Arctic waters.

Courtesy MacGillivray Freeman Films.

▲ As sea ice retreats due to climate change, polar bears must swim longer distances to reach solid ice or land. Beaufort Sea, Alaska.

► Austfonna is the third-largest ice field in the world. It covers 3,200 square miles and stretches 112 miles along the east coast of Nordaustlandet in Svalbard, Norway.

◄◄ A walrus rests on some of the last remaining summer ice off the northern coast of Svalbard, Norway.

▲ Walruses hollow out a resting place on a sandy spit on the island of Prins Karls Forland. Svalbard, Norway.

▲ A young Arctic fox investigates the area around its den. Svalbard, Norway.

▶ Huge colonies of little auk make nests in the steep rocky cliffs of Svalbard's fjords. Norway.

▲ A polar bear mother has just arrived at the shore of Hudson Bay in the middle
of July. Earlier breakup of ice in Hudson Bay is forcing bears ashore sooner.

▲ Polar bear cubs learn by imitating their mothers. Having returned to shore, they must now survive the summer months on stored fat. Hudson Bay, Canada.

►► Following pages: At the end of August the nights become dark again. Under the Big Dipper the first northern lights display their amazing light show. / Musk ox at sunrise. North Slope, Alaska.

AUTUMN

INTO THE DARKNESS

With the return of colder nights, the green hues of the tundra change to bright reds interwoven with irregular yellow lines that reveal where willows grow along the creekbeds. Flocks of snow geese fly in formation over the tundra, heading south. The cranes follow; their calls often can be heard long before the eye detects them. Caribou return south over the mountains, retreating from the advance of winter. The bulls now are carrying impressive antlers as they prepare for the rut. They are at their prime of the year as they face their rivals, fighting over the cows.

The arc of the sun drops closer to the horizon, and the first shows of the northern lights appear. From one day to the next, a snowstorm turns the landscape white. The fur on musk oxen, foxes, and bears grows thicker, and ptarmigan, Arctic fox, and Arctic hare even change their color to snow-white to blend in with their environment. The importance of the Arctic as a nesting ground can now be seen in the temperate zones as millions of geese and shorebirds migrate south, visiting the wildlife refuges along the way. Now only the year-round residents prevail in the Arctic. Ptarmigan begin to flock together in groups and feed on willow leaves along the creeks.

One animal seems eager for the return of the deeper cold of the coming winter—the polar bear. The bears rest at the edge of the Arctic Ocean, awaiting the return of the ice so they can head out to hunt for seals once again. Pregnant polar bear mothers, however, are waiting for deep enough snow to dig their maternity dens, where they will give birth to their cubs. In late winter they will emerge with their young to hunt on the ice, and the ancient cycle will continue.

◄ The northern lights break the darkness over the Tombstone Range. Yukon, Canada.

▲ A northern hawk owl scans the area for small birds and rodents. Brooks Range, Alaska.

▲ A grizzly bear wanders through a willow thicket on a foggy morning. National Petroleum Reserve, Alaska.

▶ Dall sheep at the edge of a cliff overlooking the Alaska Range.

► Wolves near the Alaska Range watch attentively as a new wolf approaches the pack.

▲ Caribou migrate over the coastal flats of the Arctic National Wildlife Refuge.

▲ A musk ox bull charges across the tundra to round up its females. North Slope, Alaska.

NORTHERN LIGHTS

My childhood thoughts and imagination often wandered off into the northern wilderness. I longed to see remote corners of the earth, explore wilderness areas with their abundance of wildlife, and experience nature's wonders. It was this longing for such places that created my passion for photographing them.

Wrapped in a thick down parka, I am lying next to Emil in the snow near the Arctic Circle, staring into the clear, starry skies, full of anticipation. I am waiting for one of the wonders I dreamed about as a child: the aurora borealis—the northern lights.

At this moment, triggered by an enormous eruption on the sun, a cosmic tsunami is heading for Earth at an astronomical speed—more than 1.8 million miles an hour. I am waiting for it to collide with our atmosphere and unleash an enormous celestial fireworks display above my head. But as I stare into the dark infinity, the sky remains black, and only the sparkle of the stars tells me that there is something else out there. Time passes. My thoughts drift away into the expanse until my mind cannot grasp the magnitude of time and space anymore. I begin to wonder, Where does space end? And if it ends, what is concealed beyond this end? In this never-ending circle of my mind, I find something divine.

Above, a satellite glides along its orbit. I think about how the entire planet is constantly being studied, assessed, recorded, and measured. It is this urge to explain, to calculate, and to predict

everything, I think, that causes us to lose our ability to wonder.

My eyes follow the satellite, but my gaze is suddenly interrupted as a huge column of light flares up from the horizon. In seconds it unfolds in a glorious burst of color. With a magnificent surge, the aurora shoots across the entire sky. In the dancing lights, the protective skin of our planet becomes visible. Like living plasma, it begins to pulsate—sometimes in slow motion, then lightning fast. Dancing, flickering, it seems to be breathing as it expands and collapses upon itself. The magic of the living lights captivates me. I tell Emil, "According to a Native tale, the earth ends at an enormous abyss, over which a small and dangerous path leads to heaven. The souls of the deceased need to travel over this path, and the ghosts of the afterworld light the way for the newcomers."

In the frozen silence I can hear my pulse in my ears. Then Emil whispers to me, "Can you hear them?" I shake my head. It seems as if I should be able to hear something so big. It's like a massive storm, yet there is just a faint crackling and humming. I think about the stories told to me by Native guides. In those tales, they say that the sounds that acompany the aurora are spirits seeking to communicate with the living. One should always answer them with a whispering voice, my guides have told me. As I listen, I cannot help but whisper back to the dancing aurora, the wonder of the Arctic.

◄ The aurora borealis, known as the northern lights, swirls through the sky over Wapusk National Park, Canada.

▶ Tombstone Range. Yukon, Canada.

▶ ▶ Following pages: As the weather turns colder, a polar bear drinks from a freshwater pool, awaiting the return of the sea ice at the edge of the Beaufort Sea, Alaska. / Polar bears that have been on shore for months with little food await formation of sea ice that will allow them to hunt for seals. Hudson Bay, Canada.

From the valleys of Yellowstone to the Utah desert and the mountains of Washington State, I have hiked and paddled the most incredible landscapes of the American West. All my adult life I have fought to preserve the wilderness treasures on our public lands.

Yet all of this did not prepare me for my first glimpse of the Arctic. In the late 1990s, as our small bush plane headed north over Achilik Pass in Alaska's Brooks Range, we followed the Achilik River. This was the largest expanse of wilderness I had ever seen—the vastness stunned me. Then, all at once, thousands of caribou appeared below us, heading up the river as they have for tens of thousands of years. They had migrated thousands of miles from the Canadian Yukon on their journey to calve in the Arctic National Wildlife Refuge, in one of the last unimpeded land migrations left on planet Earth.

After we landed, I looked north to the Arctic Ocean and the coastal plain of the Arctic Refuge. I could see for miles: no trees, just tundra and the greening of willows along the river. Through my binoculars, I spotted a wolf—far off, oblivious to me—a rare treat in the Lower 48, but common in the Arctic. The light was astounding; it never gets dark this far north in the summer.

I split off from my friends to explore a ridge by myself. Up a thousand feet, I could see the ice pack on the Arctic Ocean ten to fifteen miles away, with the shimmer of light that the heat brings. And then again, the caribou. Completely covering the landscape, thousands of caribou passed below me. The longer I looked, the more caribou I saw. I felt "pre-man"—without technology and smart phones, in a place where things never change, except with the seasons. On that day, this place became a part of me.

Will this be left for future generations, or destroyed for short-term gains for a few?

Drilling for oil in the Arctic Refuge would provide Americans with six months of oil; it is not a solution. America has 3 percent of the world's population and uses 25 percent of the world's oil—and has maybe 2 percent of the world's oil. We will never be able to drill our way to energy independence. People chanting "drill, baby, drill" have no imagination. Unless we have a broader, long-term vision and start supporting research and development of alternative energy and more efficient ways to use cars and other machines that burn oil, we will defeat ourselves. It's within our grasp to make this happen; creative innovation is a long-standing American tradition.

Over the last fifteen years, I have taken many people up to Alaska's Arctic. Politicians, writers, journalists, and photographers have brought the story home. I've supported books that bring this place to life; one was held up on the Senate floor and helped defeat a vote to drill. As executive producer of *To The Arctic*, the film on which this book is based, I hope that more people will be able to see this place as I have—and be willing to let their elected officials know that it matters. Will this precious land be left for future generations, or destroyed to create short-term gains for a few? On three occasions since the year 2000, grassroots efforts have stopped proposals to drill in the Arctic Refuge by burning up senators' phone lines and holding their feet to the fire. Now, again, is the time to become excited and engaged. The process actually works—when enough people care.

___

Tom Campion is the founder of Zumiez, an international chain of retail action-sport stores, and cofounder of the Campion Foundation. He is the chair of Alaska Wilderness League, a nonprofit group working to protect America's public lands in Alaska. Visit www.AlaskaWild.org for more information on how you can help.

◄ Thousands of Porcupine caribou graze in the shadow of Mount Michelson in the Brooks Range. Arctic National Wildlife Refuge, Alaska.

▲▲ An ice raft under the midnight sun on the Beaufort Sea. ▲ A short-eared owl hunts over the Alaskan tundra. ◄ An Arctic wolf in the Arctic National Wildlife Refuge, Alaska.

AN INTERVIEW with the PHOTOGRAPHER, FLORIAN SCHULZ

What did you hope to achieve with this book, and how did that play into how you chose to photograph the Arctic?

My overall goal was to produce a visual account of the Arctic that would bring the ecosystem to life. I wanted viewers to be able to feel what I felt when I was out in the Arctic landscape. In order to achieve this, I tried to make the wildlife part of the picture whenever possible, using wide-angle lenses or shooting in a panorama format with midrange or telephoto lenses to incorporate the animals. The panorama format also lends itself beautifully to this particular landscape. In these shots I used a video tripod so I could level out the tripod head for a straight horizon. This allowed me to rotate the camera and keep a series of images in line, which allowed for easy stitching later. Getting close to animals with the wide-angle lens was trickier, of course, especially with polar bears. For the bears I worked with remote cameras and protective cases for the camera body.

How do you get to remote Arctic locations?

Most of the time I would take a jet as far north as possible, then transfer to a small prop plane. From this point, I would jump between small Native communities on prop planes with as few as fifteen people on them. These planes often would be the only transportation between the Native settlements in the far north. Our final destination in the Arctic was usually a small Native community.

Is this where you began your expeditions?

Yes, these small communities are where the last expedition preparations were done and the travel routes were decided based on the weather or the ice conditions. Working with local guides was essential because of their intimate knowledge of the area and the wildlife. I became very sensitive to the way my guides paid close attention to the weather, noticing subtle changes and predicting storms long before they hit.

How did you travel out on the sea ice?

I've traveled thousands of miles on snowmobiles, but it was particularly meaningful when I was able to work with guides who used traditional dogsleds. I specifically recall traveling for hundreds of miles in the north of Greenland with sleds pulled by fifteen dogs. The guides were able to maneuver the sleds just by calling out short commands to the dogs.

What do you eat while on an expedition in the Arctic?

Forget fresh fruits or vegetables. When you're out in the Arctic, all of the food is as frozen as if you had taken it out of an ice chest. Eating in the Arctic centers around boiling water, with which you prepare food. You also have to store water in thermoses to keep it from freezing instantly.

I bring things like rice and oatmeal that will expand with water, but on the other hand, I have eaten traditional foods that my guides have shared with me, such as musk oxen,

Clockwise from upper left: Midnight sun throws the shadow of the photographer onto an iceberg, Baffin Island, Canada. Florian and Emil travel with sled dogs in northern Greenland. Florian's Inuit guide, Simon, leads his dogs to shore in the Nares Strait off the coast of Greenland. Florian, guarding against polar bears at night, armed with a rifle, Svalbard, Norway. Florian seeks a low perspective while photographing seals in Greenland. Looking for polar bear tracks along the glacier walls in Svalbard, Norway.

caribou, seals, arctic char, snow goose, narwhal, and beluga.

There are small stores in the Native communities that sell canned foods and other things that can be found in a supermarket, but they're very expensive and the Inuit prefer to eat the food the land provides.

Did you ever have the chance to accompany the Inuit on a hunt?

I had the opportunity to go along on a musk ox hunt with the Inuit in Greenland. We went out on traditional dogsleds. Each sled had fifteen sled dogs—we needed enough dogs to pull the sleds when they were heavy with meat from the hunt. This particular time, the Inuit brought back four musk oxen to share within the community.

What is it like to camp in polar bear country?

Quite challenging! When you're inside your tent, you are always aware that at any moment a bear might come right through the side. Someone always has to be on watch, which is fine when you're in a large group, but can be really hard when there are just two of you, as is frequently the case with me because I'm often with only a guide or my wife. When it's your turn to go on watch and you have to crawl out of a warm sleeping bag to head out into the cold, it becomes a mental battle between you and your exhaustion. Sometimes when I'm worn down by the cold and by sleep deprivation, I just want to stay in bed, polar bears or not.

What is the closest you've ever been to a polar bear?

On one occasion, a very determined polar bear came within fifteen feet of me and my guide. Its eyes had a special expression that went beyond curiosity. They looked hungry. I was preoccupied with taking frame-filling images of the polar bear that would communicate this expression when my guide realized there was no more time to spare and decided to shoot a flare. No bear had ever come that close to either me or my guide, who has lived in the Arctic for many years.

What can you do to scare a polar bear away?

They don't scare very easily, that's for sure. This is one big difference between polar bears and grizzlies. Most polar bears are simply not intimidated by humans, even if you wave your arms and yell. They also can be very curious animals. If they spot a camp from the distance, they may come straight in your direction to check it out. One time we had a whole polar bear family head straight for our camp. They first circled around us until they caught our scent on the wind, and then they came right into the middle of our camp. Raising our voices did not impress them in the least. It took one of the Inuit hunters to shoot into the air to chase them away. That's why either my guide or I carry a rifle and flare gun.

What's in your camera bag when you're out there?

For cameras I carry a Nikon D7000, a Nikon D3s, and a Nikon D3x. My lenses are the Nikon 14–24 mm, 24–70 mm, 28–70 mm, 70–200 mm f/2.8, 200–400 mm f/4, 600 mm f/4, 16 mm f/2.8 fisheye, and 24 mm tilt-shift; and I use the 1.4x teleconverter. Other equipment includes remote camera boxes, Manfrotto and Gitzo tripods, a PocketWizard for my remote setups, a Subal underwater housing, rollable solar panels, sixteen Li-ion batteries, a Nikon GPS, an Apple MacBook Pro, over 200 GB of CompactFlash cards, and three Western Digital 500GB pocket drives.

What were some of the challenges you faced working in the Arctic environment?

Hunting for incredible light, a photographer gets very little sleep in the Arctic between late spring and early fall. As the sun does not set

Clockwise from upper left: Florian checks the remote camera, Svalbard, Norway. The photographer's dream comes true as the male polar bear enters the frame. An enormous bear investigates the casing that protects the camera inside it. Curious about the noise, a polar bear takes a peek into the camera lens.

To get intimate photographs of the polar bears that had congregated at the fin whale carcass, Florian needed to get closer than the boat from which he had been watching the bears for days. He wanted to create an image that would tell the story of the bears in connection with the whale carcass and the dramatic Arctic landscape. In order to achieve such an image, the camera needed to be extremely close.

When the bears dispersed into the mountains during high tide, Florian had a few moments to set up a camera, inside a protective casing, near the whale carcass. He carefully composed a shot that included the whale carcass and the glacier in the background, leaving space for the imaginary bear.

As the tide dropped and the bears returned, Florian was standing by on a Zodiac boat with the remote trigger in hand. His careful preparation, and a bit of luck, brought the cover image of this book to life.

during these seasons, the best light often is found in the middle of the night. I frequently needed to switch my entire schedule around, sleeping during the middle of the day and then photographing throughout the night. As the light is still good in the morning or afternoon, it does not take long until one gets very sleep deprived.

Working in extremely cold conditions was particularly challenging. I created a layering system of gloves, wearing very thin undergloves, then midweight gloves, and added heavy-duty mittens on top. I often took the two heavier layers off to access small buttons on the camera. When my fingers were so badly frozen that I could not stand it any longer, I would put my mittens back on and beat my hands against my body until my fingers would work again. Wind, of course, makes the situation much worse than the cold alone.

What about your camera equipment? How did it perform in the extreme cold?

Well, the first trick is to never press your nose against the metal part of the camera, because it will quickly freeze to it! As far as how the equipment worked in the cold, I found that my cameras did fine to about -20 degrees Fahrenheit. Of course, the batteries drained faster and the cameras responded more slowly, but overall they performed well. I always kept my extra batteries close to my body so that I had a fresh, warm set whenever I needed them.

Do you need to keep the cameras themselves warm, too?

A mistake many newcomers to the Arctic make is that they keep their camera underneath their parka. *No!* Bad idea. The camera will fog up completely and be unusable. When I head out into the field, I let the cameras freeze and then remain frozen. If I need to bring the cameras inside a warm room or a heated tent, I put everything into an airtight plastic bag and let it warm to the ambient temperature before I take it out of the bag.

What was it like working with the MacGillivray Freeman film team?

Creating a companion book for a giant-screen film was a perfect match for my style of photography because I like to capture the animals in connection with the surrounding landscape. Because the filmmakers shoot images for a giant screen, they compose a lot of their imagery in a similar fashion—with large landscape shots that show animals in relation to their environment.

Of course I was very excited to work with some of the premier cinematographers in the field—sharing ideas and experiences with people such as Howard Hall and Bob Cranston as well as Shaun and Greg MacGillivray.

On some occasions you dove with the film team. How dangerous is it to dive in the Arctic Ocean?

On one hand you're confronted with water that is below freezing, around 29 degrees. The only reason it's not solid is because of the salt content in the sea water.

The cold water can cause the regulator to freeze, and air can start shooting out of your mouth piece. Because of the danger of hypothermia, you have to pay close attention to your overall body condition. Even though you're wearing a dry suit, your face and head are exposed to the freezing water, and you lose a lot of energy this way. When you're in the water diving or snorkeling, your lips and mouth freeze. When you are in the water for up to an hour, you come out and talk with a slur—it's the same feeling as if you were at the dentist and he numbed your whole mouth. You have no control because the nerves aren't functioning.

The other danger is that if you enter through a hole in the ice, you have to make sure to find your way back to the hole. In an ideal situation, someone is monitoring a rope to pull you back to the surface. If the person holding onto the rope doesn't watch closely, you could be trapped under the ice.

Top to bottom: Brad Ohlund and Zach Grant of the film team film a group of walruses; The MacGillivray Freeman film team films the glacial landscape of northwestern Svalbard. A large male polar bear wanders by the MacGillivray Freeman film team.

While diving in the Arctic Ocean, Florian photographed the undersides of icebergs, beluga whales swimming in pods, and thick-billed murres diving for food. He dove with the MacGillivray Freeman film team in Arctic water as cold as 29 degrees Fahrenheit, just below freezing. The sea water stays liquid at this temperature only because it has a very high salt content. To capture the underwater images, Florian wore a dry suit, neoprene gloves, and regulators adjusted for cold-water diving. He placed his camera in carefully constructed protective underwater housing. He paid special attention to the greasing of the O-rings used to seal the casing. In extreme cold temperatures the materials used to enclose the camera can shrink and cause a leak that could destroy the camera.

How much patience did it take to create your photographic account of the Arctic?

In serious wildlife photography, your patience is often tested. For years I returned to the Arctic just to find the large caribou herds, never mind getting the caribou images I envisioned. It took me years to even see my first polar bear, and I spent over seventy-two hours in a blind to photograph the snowy owls in this book. But, even when I'm not getting perfect images, I am learning so much about the landscape and the wildlife. So I cannot say that I'm bored waiting; I'm excited to be out in the wilderness.

You mentioned waiting for the caribou herds. What was it like when you finally saw them?

It was like a dream come true when the caribou suddenly appeared.

As a child, I envisioned the millions of bison roaming the Great Plains. These great herds have disappeared, but in the far north, millions of caribou still roam. They are a symbol for me of the wilderness areas I am trying to help protect with my photography.

As a wildlife photographer you see animals in many difficult situations. What made you decide to step in to help the caribou calf that had lost its mother?

In the course of a week, over 60,000 caribou crossed the river by our

Clockwise from upper left: Florian used a camouflage blind to photograph snowy owls without being seen. Base camp along the Utukok River in the National Petroleum Reserve, Alaska. Emil carries the rescued calf toward its mother. Florian and the Super Cub airplane during an aerial expedition. Florian and Emil on the lookout for caribou in the Western Arctic of Alaska. Florian surrounded by thousands of mosquitoes during the Arctic summer.

Whenever possible, Florian's wife, Emil Herrera Schulz, accompanies him into the field. For Florian and Emil, creating conservation photography projects is much more than a job—it's a way of life. Florian is away from home for much of the year, spending eight to ten months in the field. While on expeditions together, Emil and Florian have been challenged by extreme cold temperatures, giant swarms of mosquitoes, and long stretches without showers, but have also experienced the joy of seeing a vast herd of caribou pass their tent and watching polar bears on the ice.

Florian and Emil work closely together to create powerful visuals for books, magazines, and the live multimedia presentations they give to audiences across the United States and Europe. Emil is involved in the creation of the still images, video footage, and sound recordings that play an important role in their work.

camp. Unavoidably, caribou calves got separated from their mothers, ran around lost, or even drowned in the water. I remember a particular moment when a caribou baby ran up to me and Emil, without fear, looking for help because it thought we might be its mother. This was when I just couldn't pretend not to feel anything for these orphaned calves.

When Emil found the calf that she is holding in the photograph trapped in a mudhole, she believed she saw its mother and that we could actually reunite the two. We lifted the calf out of the mud and brought it in the direction of the frantic mother that we saw running around. Once they heard each other's calls, they ran to each other and were reunited.

I'm aware that nature needs to take its path, and that the caribou might have died and become food for a grizzly bear, but it was difficult to ignore my own emotion. The emotion I felt for this caribou calf reminded me that if we could all feel this strongly toward wildlife in a more abstract way, we might take more care of their habitat and give them this room to live.

You have a lot of aerial images in the book. How did you go about getting them?

I organized an entire Arctic aerial expedition. The key was finding a slow-flying airplane that would have a long range, and a pilot who was willing to go out with me for several weeks. The perfect match was my friend Ken McDonald, a fantastic pilot and airplane mechanic who took me out on a World War II Super Cub—a two-seater plane that can land just about anywhere (with the right pilot). We landed and camped on riverbeds and the shores of the Arctic Ocean, lifting up into the air whenever the weather was fair. The aerial perspective allowed me to show the vastness of the Arctic landscape. Through this perspective you understand that there aren't just 100, or 500, but tens of thousands of caribou migrating across the Arctic tundra.

What signs of climate change have you witnessed?

Unfortunately, I have witnessed dramatic changes in the short time—ten years—that I have been traveling to the Arctic. On land, the permafrost is melting at an unprecedented rate. During my aerial expeditions I was shocked to see the Arctic Ocean west of Barrow completely ice free at the beginning of July, as well as many areas where entire hillsides had come down in giant mudslides, taking all the vegetation with them.

From elders in different Native communities, I have heard the same story of shockingly accelerated change. The time when hunters can travel on the sea ice has been significantly reduced, and the dangers have increased. I experienced this myself on my 1,200-mile trek across Baffin Island. Many areas had dangerous ice that was too thin for safe passage.

What impact do these changes have on the wildlife?

Without ice, seals and walrus need to spend more energy moving between their resting areas and feeding grounds. Polar bears are dependent on the sea ice for their food, too—mainly ringed seals— and are under increasing pressure, which is why they are a symbol in the fight against global warming.

Caribou are affected by winter rainstorms, as a thick layer of ice prevents them from reaching food below the snow. Increasingly regular tundra fires destroy vast areas of their summer feeding ground.

The warming trend also means that wildlife species are pushing north. Moose, for example, are seen more often now in the Arctic plains due to changing vegetation. And we will also see many more species of fish in Arctic waters as the temperature warms.

The Arctic is very scarcely populated, and very few people ever visit. Why should the rest of

Above: The massive Red Dog mining operation is positioned in the middle of the migration route of the Western Arctic caribou herd.
Below: One of the oil facilities in Prudhoe Bay, just west of the Arctic National Wildlife Refuge in Alaska. Despite strict regulations, it is difficult to avoid contamination of the land, sea, and air from the oil facilities.

the world be concerned about the changes in the far north?

We need to see the world more as a whole. The Arctic ecosystem is very much a part of the rest of the world. Millions of birds and several species of whales migrate past our latitudes to the south, where they spend the winter each year. On a larger scale, we need to see the Arctic as an "air conditioner" for the world. Without the cooling effect of the Arctic on the atmosphere, we are experiencing disasters around the world like tornadoes, hurricanes, major floods, and droughts with greater frequency and of greater intensity.

Given all of this, can anything be done to slow climate change?

One major way to reduce warming in the Arctic is to cut black carbon emissions globally. My conservation partner, Earthjustice, is fighting to achieve this goal. Black carbon reduction would have a very quick effect, as it can leave the atmosphere in a matter of weeks. Of course, reducing CO_2 emissions needs to be the number one priority, and it can be achieved through improved technology and partnerships with the major stakeholders.

Most of the Arctic is so remote and inaccessible; it would not seem to lend itself to industrial development.

Unfortunately, prices for natural resources have increased dramatically over the past years, making exploitation attractive to corporations even in remote areas. There are enormous amounts of resources, from minerals to coal and oil, stored in the Arctic. With the Arctic Ocean increasingly ice free, the Arctic is more accessible to ships. I have seen hundreds of miles of tracks from seismic testing crossing the Arctic tundra and mining operations like the Red Dog Mine—a massive scar right across the migration route of the Western Arctic caribou herd.

The fight over the Arctic National Wildlife Refuge has been going

on for a long time. Why is it so important to keep this area protected?

In the Alaskan Arctic, the refuge is probably the greatest mix of stunning landscape with many different types of habitat, and presents the most spectacular array of Arctic wildlife in a relatively compact area. It is also of fundamental importance to the Porcupine caribou herd, which has migrated across the refuge for thousands of years.

How much impact does the oil industry have in the Alaskan Arctic?

To be honest, I was shocked at the size of the Prudhoe Bay oilfield when I saw it from the air. We flew for almost an hour over pump stations, oil facilities, pipelines, and roads. That being said, I have to say that in Alaska I have seen the oil industry making a very serious effort to abide by environmental regulations. They are not interested in bad publicity. Unfortunately, accidents happen nevertheless. Major oil spills have occurred along the Alaska pipeline because the pipeline walls have corroded.

In the Gulf of Mexico, there are thousands of offshore oil wells. Why is oil drilling in the Arctic Ocean such a big deal?

As we saw with the Gulf oil spill in 2010, major disasters can happen. It took many weeks to get the situation under control in the Gulf, even under fairly modest weather conditions and with great infrastructure in place.

Now think of an oil spill in the Arctic Ocean, where for months out of the year darkness and extreme cold temperatures are the norm, and there is no infrastructure—no ports or access for possible cleanup crews. To date, there is no known method to clean up an oil spill in icy waters. The entire Arctic Ocean ecosystem could be destroyed, and animals from the little krill to seals and polar bears could be heavily affected and possibly wiped out.

Migrating snow geese. Western Arctic.

Given all you have seen, what are your thoughts on climate change?

I see a lot of forces exploiting this planet at an ever-increasing rate, even though rising average temperatures and CO_2 levels are causing climate catastrophes like the dying of the world's coral reefs, rising sea levels, hurricanes, tornadoes, widespread drought, and intense floods. These phenomena are not mere predictions anymore—we are watching them on the news. The world won't disappear, but human society will be forced to adapt, and it's likely that we will lose a large percentage of the diverse species that share the planet with us.

If life as we know it will change, do you have hope for the future?

Hope is to wish for fulfillment of dreams in the face of all life's challenges. Hope is fighting for what you dream about.

I dream that rationality will win over greed. I have faith that the human race is capable of unthinkable achievements. First, we need to recognize that environmental destruction and climate change, not terrorism or a neighboring country, are the biggest enemies of our time. We need to fight on multiple levels—through public education, through change of policy, and on the industrial level through technology and the way we consume and invest.

Often we hear the argument that the economic cost of enforcing a greener policy is too high, but scientists warn today that the price to be paid in the future will be much higher. Our children and children's children will pay this price.

As I am writing these words my wife, Emil, is carrying our first baby in her belly. It was conceived in the high Arctic of Greenland. I hope that in the years to come, I will not have to tell my son stories of a world that once was. I hope that we can continue to explore this frozen world as a family to tell the story of the Arctic. And I am fighting for this dream.

This gives me hope.

AN INTERVIEW with GREG MacGILLIVRAY and SHAUN MacGILLIVRAY, Director and Producer of *TO THE ARCTIC*

Why did you decide to make a film about the Arctic?

GREG: I've been interested in creating a film about the Arctic for more than twenty years. The wildness and grandness of the place make it the perfect subject matter for IMAX Theatres. The topic also tested extremely well with our audiences. In fact, out of twenty different topics I've tested over a fifteen-year period, the Arctic tested the highest. So I knew we would have interested fans. Then, in 2006, my friend Bobby Kennedy, Jr., called. He had just flown and rafted through the Alaskan Arctic with a man named Tom Campion, whose life mission is to save this amazing wilderness—one of our last great unspoiled regions—forever. Bobby was excited. He said, "Call Tom—he wants to help with your Arctic film!" In two weeks, Tom was my partner, matching my financial investment in the movie, dollar for dollar.

SHAUN: The Arctic is like the canary in the coal mine when it comes to climate change. The changes we're witnessing there are like a warning of the global changes to come if we don't find a way to mitigate climate change. We knew that if we could transport people to the Arctic with this film, and make them fall in love with Arctic wildlife like polar bears,

we would have a great vehicle for motivating people to become part of the solution. Through our online platform and working with our conservation partners like Alaska Wilderness League, Polar Bears International, and Oceana, we can empower people to take small, easy actions that will help protect the Arctic.

What surprised you the most about the Arctic?

GREG: Polar bear mothers have the hardest job on Earth, and the job is getting harder every day. I was so amazed and moved by the tenacity of the mother bear that let us follow her and her two cubs for nearly a week. Everything she has to do to keep herself and her cubs alive is now much more difficult because of warming temperatures. She doesn't have as many months to hunt because her hunting grounds, the sea ice platforms, are melting earlier each year. And as the ice floes shrink, she and other polar bears must occupy a smaller location, meaning there's extra competition for territory and food. And yet she never gives up. She's completely committed to her cubs' well-being and safety, twenty-four hours a day.

SHAUN: I was surprised to find the Arctic still such a truly wild, pristine place. It's one of our last true wildernesses on Earth. By getting the word out there with *To The Arctic* and with this book, we hope to help keep it that way.

While in Svalbard, Norway, you gained unprecedented filming access to a polar bear mother and her two cubs. What did it feel like to watch this family for those several days?

GREG: It was an honor felt by all twenty-one members of our team. Never before had filmmakers tracked a polar bear family at such close range twenty-four hours a

Clockwise from upper left: The MacGillivray Freeman Films production crew used a 103-foot icebreaker, the *Havsel*, as their home base while on location for twenty-two days in the archipelago of Svalbard, Norway. The icebreaker gave the film crew special access to the region's polar bears who hunt seals all summer long on the sea ice platforms, called ice floes. Unique aerial views photographed from the *Havsel's* mast reveal a great expanse of Arctic seas and the recent changes in sea ice density. The film crew traveled to within nine degrees of the North Pole. *To The Arctic* film director Greg MacGillivray (in orange jacket) and director of photography Brad Ohlund also used a small skiff to get even closer to the bears. "We were in such an exquisite, remote place, it felt like being at the end of the world," observed MacGillivray.

PHOTOS AT FAR UPPER LEFT, AND MIDDLE LEFT, ABOVE, COURTESY MACGILLIVRAY FREEMAN FILMS.

day for nearly a week. The captain of our icebreaker, who has worked in the region for thirty years, said, "This is the smartest mother bear I've ever seen. She's not wasting energy trying to get away from us, her friends. Her two cubs are super well trained; they know when to run and swim downwind to escape an attacking male bear. She knows how to catch seals and even birds. She's very clever!" After the first twenty-four-hour day of tracking the family with cameras and binoculars, we knew this was a once-in-a-lifetime experience.

SHAUN: Because we observed this family of bears for so long, we felt very connected to them. Their struggles to escape the male polar bears and their successes in catching seals felt like our struggles and successes. We couldn't believe how smart and dedicated this mother polar bear was. It was an experience I will never forget.

You've sent IMAX cameras to the top of Mount Everest and all around the world. How did the Arctic challenge your film team?

GREG: In the Arctic, we were filming wildlife, which is very difficult to film, especially in such harsh conditions. There is a lot of waiting and searching for the animals, and then you want to try to capture a variety of animal behaviors. We were in the field much longer for *To The Arctic* than for any of our other films, including *Everest*.

SHAUN: It was colder, wetter—and smellier! The showers on our icebreaker weren't working, so for three weeks we didn't bathe. At least at Everest Base Camp, you can have a solar-heated shower once a week if you have the energy to do so.

The underwater footage in the film is amazing. Diving under the ice in extreme temperatures with an IMAX camera must be incredibly difficult. And how did you get shots of the mother polar bear and cubs swimming above and approaching the camera?

To The Arctic cameraman Bob Cranston and filmmaker Adam Ravetch maneuver the giant IMAX camera in Arctic Bay, Canada, in water literally as cold as ice. The salt content allows it to remain liquid, even though the water temperature is below freezing. COURTESY DALE SANDERS/MACGILLIVRAY FREEMAN FILMS.

above and approaching the camera? Wasn't that dangerous for the filmmakers?

GREG: That was pure Bob Cranston! Bob is a brave underwater cinematographer who has photographed alligators, great white sharks, venomous snakes, and now the fiercest predator of all—polar bears. They're eating machines. So we sent in Bob. He invented a way to shoot them by diving down deep, then waiting for the bears' natural curiosity to cause them to investigate our cameras, which gave us great shots. Fortunately, the bears don't like to dive too deep, so Bob felt relatively safe. You can watch his description of this in a video posted on our website, www.OneWorldOneOcean.org.

SHAUN: I wouldn't do what Bob did! These were dangerous conditions, but Bob is extremely experienced and well trained to film in all kinds of difficult situations. Because of the extreme water temperatures, which were below freezing, Bob's longest dive under the ice was forty-five minutes. Any longer and his hands would have become completely frozen.

Florian Schulz accompanied you on some of the film shoots. How do you compare/contrast his still photography and passion for the Arctic and what you were trying to accomplish as filmmakers?

GREG: Florian is the rare still photographer who, like our production team, thinks about images twenty-four hours a day. When you're passionate about doing something better than anyone has done it before, you're up early, always on the alert, always engaged and thinking up "what ifs." That's why Florian fit in so well with our team—and got such incredible shots.

SHAUN: Florian knows how to get that one perfect still image that captures the essence of a place or an animal. It was a joy working with him. He is incredibly talented, very passionate, and a good friend.

What have you learned about the Arctic that was most impressive or memorable, not as a filmmaker but as someone who has had a unique opportunity to visit and experience this faraway place?

GREG: Everyone knows that the planet is changing, but what they don't know that the Arctic is changing three times faster. For the glaciers, the ice cap, the animals, and the Native people, these changes are bringing hardship. Can we help? Yes, we can. But first, more people have to become aware of what's happening. That's where our film and this book come in, as well as what Coca-Cola and World Wildlife Fund are doing with their Arctic Home campaign, and the wonderful work of our other partners, too. If enough people fall in love with the Arctic and support conservation efforts, we can make a difference.

SHAUN: When you're there in the Arctic, you get this incredible sense of being connected to nature and to a truly wild, expansive place. You also see how difficult survival is for the wildlife there, and how everything is interconnected. If you alter one thing in that "web of life," it has a rippling effect across the entire ecosystem. Audiences who see our film in eighty-foot-tall IMAX Theatres will feel transported. They will get that same sense of wonder and appreciation for this incredible environment that I was lucky enough to experience firsthand over the last five years.

What is your film's take-home message for audiences?

GREG: We have a very special planet. It is our duty to ourselves, to our God, and to our children's children to leave it as we found it. But as oceanographer Sylvia Earle often says, we are the lucky generation because through our recent scientific research, we now know enough to be able to preserve it.

SHAUN: We can all make a difference with small simple decisions and actions in our daily lives.

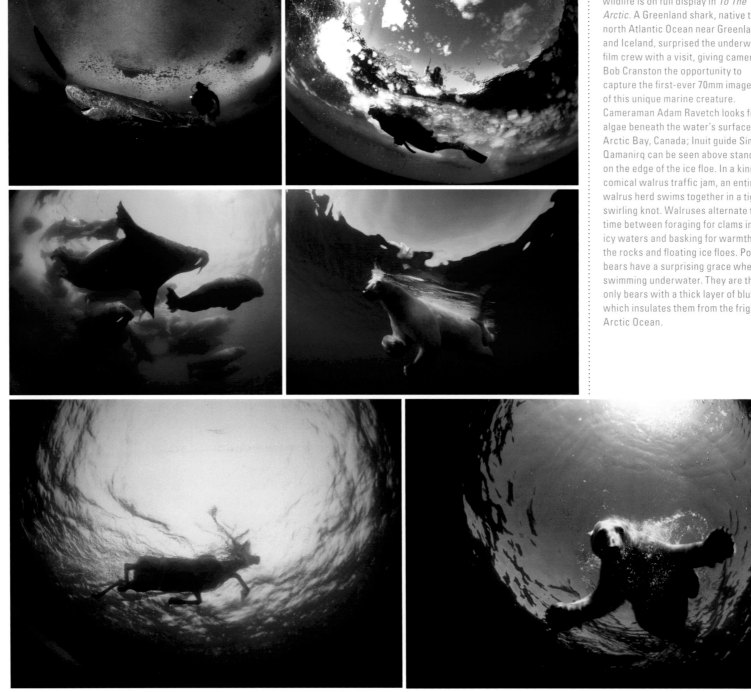

Left: The diversity of Arctic marine wildlife is on full display in *To The Arctic*. A Greenland shark, native to the north Atlantic Ocean near Greenland and Iceland, surprised the underwater film crew with a visit, giving cameraman Bob Cranston the opportunity to capture the first-ever 70mm images of this unique marine creature. Cameraman Adam Ravetch looks for algae beneath the water's surface in Arctic Bay, Canada; Inuit guide Simon Qamanirq can be seen above standing on the edge of the ice floe. In a kind of comical walrus traffic jam, an entire walrus herd swims together in a tight swirling knot. Walruses alternate their time between foraging for clams in the icy waters and basking for warmth on the rocks and floating ice floes. Polar bears have a surprising grace when swimming underwater. They are the only bears with a thick layer of blubber, which insulates them from the frigid Arctic Ocean.

To The Arctic is part of your larger One World One Ocean campaign to improve public understanding of the oceans. What is this campaign?

GREG: One World One Ocean is a nonprofit, ten-year campaign with a goal to reach and engage millions of individuals through a sustained multimedia release of giant-screen films, feature films, television programs, online initiatives, and grassroots education programs—all designed to motivate and empower people to become part of a movement to restore and protect our oceans. We have already lost 90 percent of the big fish in the ocean due to overfishing. Less than 2 percent of the ocean is protected in marine sanctuaries and reserves (in comparison, more than 12 percent of our planet's land resources are protected in national parks and refuges). Our three simple, yet important campaign goals are to support international efforts to protect 10 percent of the ocean by 2020, to inspire people to eat seafood more sustainably, and to reduce plastic marine debris. If we are able to achieve these goals by 2020, scientists feel that the ocean will have the chance to rebound and thrive.

SHAUN: We're also trying to build a web-based community of fifteen million new ocean fans, whom we will direct to our conservation partners who are already driving conservation policy and change. We are in a unique position to build this community because of the reach of our giant-screen films, which play at more than two hundred IMAX Theatres and other giant-screen cinemas in thirty-two countries. Our hope is that once we engage people emotionally through our films, they'll want to make the social changes necessary to save and restore our oceans.

You can learn more by visiting www.OneWorldOneOcean.org.

Opposite page: In a scene from *To The Arctic*, a walrus dives down to inspect the IMAX camera—and warn off the underwater film crew. Mother walrus teach their young survival skills, such as scaring off intruders. As the film crew recorded walrus behavior underwater, protective mothers would steer their curious pups away. Above from left to right: While filming polar bears underwater near Baffin Island, Canada, cameraman Bob Cranston got lucky when a caribou entered the water and swam across the inlet, providing a unique underwater shot from below. To capture underwater footage of the polar bears, Cranston would dive deeper than polar bears are comfortable diving, then slowly rise to within a safe distance. The bears' natural curiosity made for some cute close-ups. If ever a bear got too close for comfort, Bob would quickly descend farther.

Photos on pages 206 and 207 courtesy MacGillivray Freeman Films.

MACGILLIVRAY FREEMAN'S
TO THE ARCTIC

A One World One Ocean Foundation presentation of a MacGillivray Freeman Films Production.

Produced with support provided by Campion Foundation, Reynders, McVeigh Capital Management, Canadian Museum of Civilization, MacGillivray Freeman Films Educational Foundation and One World One Ocean Foundation in association with Oceana, Alaska Wilderness League, and Polar Bears International.

Produced by
MacGillivray Freeman Films,
Laguna Beach

Directed by
Greg MacGillivray

Produced by
Shaun MacGillivray

Executive Producers
Tom Campion for Campion
Foundation
Chat Reynders

**Music Score Composed and
Arranged by**
Steve Wood

Written by
Stephen Judson

**Baffin Island and Hudson Bay
Sequences Directed by**
Adam Ravetch

Directors of Photography
Brad Ohlund
Bob Cranston

Aerial Photography
Ron Goodman, Cinematographer
Phil Rothwell
Spacecam Systems

Cinematographers
Greg MacGillivray
Jack Tankard
Bob Cranston
Howard Hall
Brad Ohlund
Rob Walker
Shaun MacGillivray

**Underwater Photography Unit:
Director of Photography/
Underwater Cinematographer**
Robert Cranston
Howard Hall
Support Diver
Dale Sanders

Edited by
Stephen Judson

Associate Editor
Robert Walker

Post-Production Coordinator
Matthew Muller

Senior Producer
Harrison Smith

Associate Producers
Kathy Almon
Daniel White
Patty Collins

Science Advisory Panel
Steven Amstrup, PhD,
Senior Scientist, Polar Bears
International
Dr. Ian Stirling, PhD,
Adjunct Professor, Department
of Biological Sciences,
University of Alberta
Andrew E. Derocher, PhD,
Professor, Department of
Biological Sciences, University
of Alberta
Chris Krenz, PhD,
Arctic Project Manager, Oceana,
Pacific Office

In Promotional Partnership with
Coca-Cola Company
Canadian Museum of Civilization

Featuring
Karsten Heuer
Leanne Allison
Adam Ravetch,
Co-Director of the Arctic
Sequences; Field Producer;
Cinematographer
Simon Qamanirq

1st Assistant Cameraman
Robert Walker
Jack Tankard
Russell Bowie
Zach Grant

Still Photographers
Florian Schulz
Barbara MacGillivray
Shaun MacGillivray

Script Researchers and Treatments
Katie MacGillivray
Meghan MacGillivray
Janna Emmel

Production Assistants
Cindy Olson
Susan Wilson

Location Manager
Jason Roberts

On-Location Assistants
Cooper Ravetch
Sarah Robertson
Rosie Robertson
Jon Waterman
Odd Magne Kvalshagenn
Steinar Aksnej
Arne Sivertsen
Captain Bjorne
Jason Issigiatok

Alaska Air Services
Coyote Air, Dirk Nickisch and
Danielle Tirrell

Sales and Marketing
Chip Bartlett
Alice Casbara-Leek
Bob Harman
Mike Lutz
Jamie Hinrichs

Sponsorship
Patty Collins
Mary Jane Dodge
Keri Salemme

**Public Relations/
Book Project Supervisor**
Lori Rick

Accounting
Jeff Horst
Jennifer Leininger
Debbie Bergin
Victoria Stokes

Post Production Consultants
David Keighley Productions
70mm Inc.

**Stereo Conversion & Digital Visual
Effects**
Sassoon Film Design

Supervising Producer
Tim Sassoon

Executive Producer
Jenn Bastian

Digital Stereographer
Chie Yoshii

**Opening and End Titles, Digital
Visual Effects, and S3D
Conversions Produced by**
Alan G. Markowitz
Visceral Image Productions

Visual Effects Producers
Matthew Muller
Valerie Johnson-Redrow

First Assistant Film Editor
Jason Stearns

Assistant Film Editors
Tim Amick
Toby Wallwork
Erin Hill
Jason E. Paul

Supervising Sound Editor
Andrew DeCristifaro, MPSE
Soundelux

Re-Recording Mixer
Ken Teaney CAS
Todd – AO Studios

Featured Vocalists
Ragnheiour Grondal
Beth Fitchet Wood

Stock Footage Courtesy of
National Film Board of Canada,
Being Caribou Footage
Daniel White/Big Films Inc.
Primesco
John Downer Productions Ltd.
Thought Equity Motion/BBC
Motion Gallery
Archival film from the collections
of the Library of Congress
Ole Salomonsen
Arctic Light Photo
Bob Eather/KEO Consultants

Special Thanks to
Campion Foundation
Alaska Wilderness League
Polar Bears International
Oceana
SeaWorld San Diego
Arctic Wild, LLC
Bill Mohrwinkel
Garrett Jones
Arctic Bear Productions
Beto Bedolfe
Oceana board members
Keith Addis
Jim Simon
Frontiers North
National Film Board of Canada
Leverton & Associates Ltd.
World Wildlife Fund
Patrick Klos
Mose Richards

Filmed Exclusively on
Kodak Motion Picture Film in 15/70

Color by
Technicolor®

**For more information about
this film, please visit
www.ToTheArctic.com.**

This listing does not include all
final film credits.

One World One Ocean Foundation is a nonprofit organization dedicated to radically reshaping the way people think about the ocean and inspiring much-needed change. Using the power of entertainment—film, television, and new media—and grassroots social action and education programs, One World One Ocean is launching the largest multimedia campaign of its kind. Entertainment projects include three 3D films for IMAX Theatres and other giant-screen cinemas, a television series, a 3D theatrical documentary, and a robust online platform that will serve as the hub of the campaign. One World One Ocean aims to build a community of 15 million active ocean advocates and raise more than $20 million to fund ocean conservation projects that support its campaign goals: create more marine sanctuaries, change how people eat seafood, and reduce plastic marine debris. *To The Arctic* is the first film presentation of One World One Ocean. www.oneworldoneocean.org

MACGILLIVRAY FREEMAN FILMS

MacGillivray Freeman Films is an innovative team of specialists in the development, production, and distribution of experiential films for IMAX Theatres and other giant-screen cinemas. Founded by Greg MacGillivray and the late Jim Freeman, this award-winning film production company creates positive, enriching giant-screen experiences as it explores new and more exciting ways to take audiences on an unforgettable adventure. Among the company's more than thirty giant-screen film credits are *Everest*, *Coral Reef Adventure*, *Hurricane on the Bayou*, *To Fly!*, and two Academy Award–nominated documentaries: *The Living Sea* and *Dolphins*. MacGillivray Freeman Films are known for their artistry and their celebration of the natural world. www.macfreefilms.com

This not-for-profit organization was established in 2004 by Greg and Barbara MacGillivray to produce and fund educational giant-screen films and companion programming that promote greater awareness and preservation of our planet's environmental and cultural heritage. Under the helm of foundation president Chris Palmer, the foundation supported the development of educational materials for students and the general public to accompany the release of *To The Arctic*. www.mffeducation.org

The Campion Foundation was founded in 2005 to protect wilderness, end homelessness, and build a vibrant nonprofit sector. Our approach to wilderness preservation is founded on the same principles that built the foundation's assets: leveraging resources, taking informed risks, investing in leaders, and seizing opportunities. We believe that we can achieve the greatest impact by investing in efforts to permanently protect our nation's largest remaining public lands: the wilderness areas in western North America. Our focus on America's Arctic—from the western Arctic to the Arctic National Wildlife Refuge to the Arctic Ocean—seeks to set aside these globally important ecosystems, conserving the innumerable lakes and marshes, the free-flowing rivers, and the largest concentrations of wildlife in the United States. We are proud to support Alaska Wilderness League and the partners of *To The Arctic* in this effort to protect the vast and magnificent landscape that is the Arctic. www.campionfoundation.org

Reynders, McVeigh Capital Management is a socially progressive investment management firm that believes economic success is directly tied to sustainability, long-term vision, and independent thinking in a changing world. Our clients invest in companies and projects built largely around environmental change and, of course, strong financial performance. Ranked fourteenth on *Wealth Manager* magazine's 2010 list of top wealth managers, Reynders, McVeigh leverages its proprietary research and emphasizes transparency, discretion, and a deep due diligence process in support of each investment. Reynders, McVeigh is a longtime supporter of MacGillivray Freeman Films, which plays an important role in educating current and future generations about the impact of climate change. We are proud to be a part of their captivating work. www.reyndersmcveigh.com

The Coca-Cola Company is partnering with World Wildlife Fund and MacGillivray Freeman Films to raise awareness and funds for the polar bear and its habitat. A Coca-Cola icon and beloved animal, the polar bear has meant a great deal to people around the world for decades. To learn about this effort and how you can help, visit www.ArcticHome.com. To learn more about the Company's commitment to making a positive difference in the world, visit www. sustainability.thecoca-colacompany.com.

The Canadian Museum of Civilization is the country's most important museum of human history and is an essential Canadian cultural and educational resource. It tells the story of Canada and its peoples from earliest times to the present day, from coast to coast to coast. Through its collections, exhibitions, public programs, research, and publications, the museum helps to preserve and promote the heritage of Canada for present and future generations, thereby contributing to the promotion and enhancement of a Canadian identity. The Museum of Civilization is also home to the Canadian Children's Museum, the Canadian Postal Museum, and an IMAX 3D Theatre. www.civilization.ca

ALASKA WILDERNESS LEAGUE
Your Land.
Your Voice.

Since 1993, Alaska Wilderness League has been leading the effort to preserve Alaska's wild lands and waters by engaging citizens, sharing resources, collaborating with other organizations, educating the public, and providing a courageous, constant, and victorious voice for Alaska in the nation's capital. The league is the only organization in the nation's capital dedicated solely to the preservation of Alaska's wilderness. Alaska Wilderness League is proud to partner with MacGillivray Freeman Films and The Mountaineers Books in this effort to promote conservation of the Arctic's lands and waters through *To The Arctic* and this companion book. www.alaskawild.org

Polar Bears International (PBI) is the only nonprofit organization focused solely on the worldwide conservation of the polar bear and its Arctic habitat. We champion polar bears wherever they are, concentrating our strategies in areas of research, education, and stewardship. www.polarbearsinternational.org

OCEANA | Protecting the World's Oceans

Oceana is the largest international advocacy group working solely to protect the world's oceans. Oceana wins policy victories for the oceans using science-based campaigns. Since 2001, we have protected over 1.2 million square miles of ocean, in the Arctic and elsewhere. Oceana is proud to support *To The Arctic* and the effort to highlight what is at stake in the Arctic and why it is so important we take the steps needed to protect it. www.oceana.org

World Wildlife Fund (WWF) is the world's leading conservation organization, working in one hundred countries for half a century. With the support of almost 5 million members worldwide, WWF is dedicated to delivering science-based solutions to preserve the diversity and abundance of life on Earth, halt the degradation of the environment, and combat climate change. WWF is a proud partner of MacGillivray Freeman Films and *To The Arctic*, which uses the power of IMAX film technology to educate and inspire viewers to both appreciate the Arctic and preserve it. Since 1992, WWF has worked in the Arctic to develop innovative solutions that are as adaptive and resilient as nature itself. www.worldwildlife.org

ACKNOWLEDGMENTS

The book you hold in your hands was an enormous undertaking. No project of this scale can be realized alone. My sincere gratitude goes out to the many people who helped to bring this book to life.

First and foremost, I want to thank my wife, Emil Herrera-Schulz, for her tireless support. A project like this is not a job—it is a way of life. We had to work through rough situations in the field, and then we did not see each other for many months at a time. Her positive spirit, creativity, and love for nature have fueled me in difficult times. I feel the greatest happiness doing this work with her at my side.

This book would not have been possible without the generous support of foundations and individuals who recognize the power of images in the fight for conservation. I am greatly indebted to my friends and supporters Margot MacDougall, Tom and Sonya Campion, Martha Kongsgaard, Ann and Ron Holz, and Renate Schreieck. You not only believe in my work but have become good friends over the years. I cannot thank you enough!

A very special thank-you goes to the MacGillivray Freeman Films team, who trusted my photographic eye to create the companion book to their film *To The Arctic*: Shaun and Greg MacGillivray and their many team members, including Lori Rick, Brad Ohlund, Rob Walker, Zach Grant, Howard Hall and Bob Cranston. I will carry with me many memories of our time in the field. *To The Arctic* will be seen by millions of people in IMAX Theatres around the world, which makes it a unique and powerful opportunity to educate people about the importance of the Arctic environment. My hope is that the film, along with this book, will galvanize public support for greater protection of all life in this part of the world.

I also thank the film's partners and contributors—the Campion Foundation, Reynders, McVeigh Capital Management, The Coca-Cola Company, Canadian Museum of Civilization, Alaska Wilderness League, Polar Bears International, Oceana, World Wildlife Fund, and One World One Ocean—for all they are doing to raise awareness about the Arctic. This is an impressive group of organizations who are doing invaluable work on behalf of this important region.

Special thanks to Greg MacGillivray for providing the preface to this book, and to Sylvia Earle for honoring us with a powerful introduction. My appreciation extends to Tom Campion for providing the thoughtful afterword, and for his tireless efforts to protect America's Arctic. Thank you to Wade Davis, Paul Nicklen, Joe Simon and Kathy Moran for providing blurbs for the book, and to Kathy also for working with such care as an editor on my first *National Geographic* story on polar bears. I have learned so much about the editing process while working with her.

I am also grateful for the steadfast support throughout the years of Helen Cherullo, publisher of The Mountaineers Books and executive director of Braided River. Since our first collaboration, on the book *Yellowstone to Yukon: Freedom to Roam*, Helen's vision of publishing in support of preserving wild places has continued to grow. She established the Braided River publishing imprint, as well as a nonprofit organization that advocates for conservation through combining the arts of photography and literature for books, exhibits, events, and media. Over the years we have established not only a strong working relationship but a deep friendship. I am greatly appreciative of her belief in Emil and me. Another big thank-you goes to the entire Braided River team: Janet Kimball, Margaret Sullivan, Laura Waltner, Sherri Schultz, Kate Rogers, and Emily White. My special gratitude goes to book designer Betty Watson, who put her heart and soul into this project. Not only do I love her work, but I have great respect for her tireless dedication to making this book the best it can be.

～

Photography becomes powerful as a conservation tool when it is paired with a strong conservation partner, and Earthjustice has been an exceptional partner of mine over the years. I want to thank Ray Wan, Bill Karpowicz, Buck Parker, and Trip Van Noppen for the wonderful collaboration. A special thank you also to Patagonia for helping with Earthjustice events and public outreach, as well as providing excellent winter clothes that kept me warm on many of my expeditions. The Nikon Professional Team of Germany—in particular Yasuo Baba and Michael Ramroth—provided excellent service on any equipment questions. Even in arctic winter conditions, my equipment did not let me down!

While my wife, Emil, and I often work alone, in the field I needed to work with different guides during this project. My special thanks go to my good friends and guides, Audun B. Tholfsen and Christopher Wiken, for their great companionship in the high Arctic. This was not just a job for them; they were just as passionate about wildlife as I, and never hesitated to help so I could capture in real life the images I had envisioned. I further want to thank Jason Roberts, Steinar Aksnes (for the long boat ride to pick up my lost luggage), Odd Magne Kvålshagen, Tobias Simigaq and Hans Jensen, Dexter Koonoo, Rafael, Thomas Lenartz, David Reid, and Carol Kasza and Jim Campbell, as well as the Governor of Svalbard and the Sysselmannen for granting us the permit for working in different locations in Svalbard.

Access to remote locations was often possible only with the help of experienced pilots, and for this my thanks go to Buck Maxson and Dirk Nikisch of Coyote Air. Aerial photography was especially important to fully represent the Arctic expanse of Alaska. I especially want to thank my good friend and outstanding pilot Ken MacDonald for his willingness to undertake the aerial expedition with me. We had a blast on this incredible adventure.

Many thanks to researchers Lincoln Parrett, Jim Dau, and Lori Quackenbush of the Alaska Department of Fish and Game; Denver Holt, who has dedicated his life to owl research; and Stan Senner, the former head of Audubon Alaska, who has given me valuable information on priority conservation areas.

Then there are our many friends to whom we are greatly indebted. We thank all of you for keeping our friendship alive even though we sometimes don't see each other for months or even years. This means a lot to Emil and me. We especially want to thank James Daniels and Theresa Mackey, who have provided us with a home away from home; Jon and Daisy Cornforth, Adam Weintraub, and Xiomara Romero; Kelly Walters and Carl Battreall, for not only welcoming my visits but keeping my good old VW van in Alaska; Hakon Askerhaug for our joint expeditions; and Dona and Curtis Perrin, Lynn Schooler, Shanyn Moore, and Kelly Walters for being there to listen when I went through tough times. We also thank our friends and colleagues Daniel Zatz, Susan Aikens, Robert and Claira Dirks, Bernt Rommelt, Christina Mittermeier, Darren and Rhea DeStefano, and the Poindexter family. We value your friendship tremendously.

Last but not least, I want to thank my family in Germany—my parents, Gerdi and Achim Schulz, and my siblings, Jonathan, Immanuel, Sarah, and Salomon—from the bottom of my heart for their support and for believing in our work.

 The Mountaineers Books is the nonprofit publishing arm of The Mountaineers, an organization founded in 1906 and dedicated to the exploration, preservation, and enjoyment of outdoor and wilderness areas.

1001 SW Klickitat Way, Suite 201, Seattle, WA 98134

© 2011 MacGillivray Freeman Films
Text © 2011 by Florian Schulz
Foreword © 2011 Sylvia Earle
Preface © 2011 Greg MacGillivray
Afterword © 2011 Tom Campion
Notes from the Field, MacGillivray Freeman Films
　© 2011 Greg MacGillivray and Shaun MacGillivray

Photographs © 2011 Florian Schulz, with the exception of images © 2011 MacGillivray Freeman Films on pages 83, 171, 204–207 as noted.

Publisher and Acquiring Editor: Helen Cherullo
Cover and Book Design: Elizabeth M. Watson, Watson Graphics
Developmental Editor: Janet Kimball
Managing Editor: Margaret Sullivan
Braided River Development and Communications: Laura Waltner
Copy Editor: Sherri Schultz
Cartographer: John Barnett/4 Eyes Design
Scientific Advisor: Steven C. Amstrup, Senior Scientist, Polar Bears International

Braided River would like to acknowledge Lori Rick of MacGillivray Freeman Films, Gary Hawkey of iocolor, and Emil Herrera-Schulz for their help producing this book.

Library of Congress Cataloging-in-Publication Data

Schulz, Florian, 1975-
To the Arctic / by Florian Schulz. — 1st ed.
　p. cm.
ISBN 978-1-59485-487-3
Arctic regions—Pictorial works. 2. Arctic regions—Description and travel. 3. Natural history—Arctic regions. I. Title.
G610.S38 2011
550.911'3—dc23
　　　　　　　　　　　　　　　　　　　2011030286

ISBN: 978-1-59485-487-3

Color and print management by iocolor Seattle
Printed at the Artron Color Printing Company, China
IMAX® is a registered trademark of IMAX Corporation

BRAIDED RIVER

BRAIDED RIVER, the conservation imprint of The
Mountaineers Books, combines photography and stories to
bring a fresh perspective to key environmental issues facing
western North America's last wild places. Books reach beyond
the printed page as these distinctive voices and images
encompass a wider and more diverse audience through
multimedia events and exhibits. Braided River's mission is to
build public support for wilderness preservation campaigns
and inspire public action. This work is made possible through
book sales and donor contributions made to Braided River, a
501(c)(3) nonprofit organization.

Please visit www.BraidedRiver.org for more information on
events, exhibits, speakers, and how to contribute to this work.

THE MOUNTAINEERS, founded in 1906, is a nonprofit
outdoor activity and conservation organization whose mission
is "to explore, study, preserve, and enjoy the natural beauty
of the outdoors. . . . " Based in Seattle, Washington, it is now
one of the largest such organizations in the United States, with
seven branches throughout Washington State.

The Mountaineers sponsors both classes and year-round
outdoor activities in the Pacific Northwest, which include
hiking, mountain climbing, ski-touring, snowshoeing, bicycling,
camping, canoeing and kayaking, nature study, sailing, and
adventure travel. The Mountaineers' conservation division
supports environmental causes through educational activities,
sponsoring legislation, and presenting informational programs.

THE MOUNTAINEERS BOOKS, an active, nonprofit publishing
program of The Mountaineers, produces guidebooks,
instructional texts, historical works, natural history guides,
and works on environmental conservation. All books
produced by The Mountaineers Books fulfill the mission of
The Mountaineers. Visit www.mountaineersbooks.org to find
details about all our titles and the latest author events, as well
as videos, web clips, links, and more!

Books may be purchased for corporate, educational, or other
promotional sales. For special discounts and information,
contact our sales department at (800) 553-4453 or mbooks@
mountaineersbooks.org.

**For more information on this book, partners,
events, and how you can make a difference,
please visit www.WelcometotheArctic.org.**

OTHER BRAIDED RIVER TITLES

Yellowstone to Yukon: Freedom to Roam: Photographer
Florian Schulz takes us down the spine of the Rocky
Mountains, capturing the splendors and vulnerability
of North America's grandest wildlife corridor. The book
was a winner of an Independent Publisher Book Award
as one of the ten outstanding books of the year and the
book most likely to save the planet.

The Last Polar Bear: Images of a unique and imperiled
web of life, with the polar bear at its center, by
photographer Steven Kazlowski.

*Arctic National Wildlife Refuge: Seasons of Life and
Land:* A comprehensive portrait of the Arctic National
Wildlife Refuge in fall, winter, spring, and summer.
Images by Subhankar Banerjee.

Arctic Wings: A tribute to the birds that journey to the
Arctic National Wildlife Refuge and back every year.
Images by Subhankar Banerjee and others.

Being Caribou: A journey with Karsten Heuer and
Leanne Allison as they migrate over one thousand miles
on foot with the Porcupine caribou herd through North
America's Arctic.

Planet Ice: A Climate for Change: A testament to
the power of ice and its unique role in revealing the
condition of our planet. Images by James Martin.

Ice Bear: The Arctic World of Polar Bears: A portrait of
the world of the polar bear as well as the entire Arctic
landscape. Images by Steven Kazlowski.

*Midnight Wilderness: Journeys in Alaska's Arctic
National Wildlife Refuge:* A passionate and vivid account
of one of America's greatest natural treasures, by author
Debbie Miller.

A Coca-Cola icon and World Wildlife Fund
(WWF) "flagship" species, the polar bear has
meant a great deal to people around the world
for decades. But this beloved animal and its
home are being threatened due to melting ice.
In a joint effort to call attention to the plight
of the polar bear, Coca-Cola and WWF have
launched a new initiative called Arctic Home.
Through this effort, they hope to bring the
vision of an Arctic refuge for the polar bear
to life. To learn more about how you can help
create a brighter, whiter future for the polar
bear, please visit ArcticHome.com.